Person-centred Counselling and
Christian Spirituality

ISHL

The Whurr Counselling and Psychotherapy Series seeks to publish selected works of foremost experts in the field of counselling and psychotherapy. Each volume features the best of a key figure's work, bringing together papers that have been published widely in the professional literature. In this way the work of leading counsellors and psychotherapists is being made accessible in single volumes.

Windy Dryden
Series editor

Person-centred Counselling and Christian Spirituality

The Secular and the Holy

Brian Thorne

Professorial Fellow and Director of the Centre for Counselling Studies,
University of East Anglia, Norwich

Counselling and Psychotherapy Series
Series Editor: **Windy Dryden**

Whurr Publishers
London

© 1998 Whurr Publishers Ltd
First published 1998 by
Whurr Publishers Ltd
19b Compton Terrace, London N1 2UN, England

Reprinted 2000 and 2003

British Library Cataloguing in Publication Data
A catalogue record for this book is available from the
British Library.

ISBN 1 86156 080 X

Printed and bound in the UK by Athenaeum Press Ltd,
Gateshead, Tyne & Wear

Contents

For Rex, Sub-Dean of Lincoln – vulnerable, resolute, human and holy, and in fond memory of British Rail in whose carriages most of this book was written.

Acknowledgements

I am, as always, deeply grateful to the secretaries of the University Counselling Service in the University of East Anglia for finding the time, patience and skill to word-process the contents of this book in its various stages. Most especially I wish to thank Jane Ramsbottom who has seen the manuscript through to its final form for all her meticulous care and courtesy in the midst of a frenetic administrative life.

Prologue

Not all that long ago I had the somewhat unnerving experience of being part of the subject matter for a doctoral thesis. Dr Gordon Lynch (yes, his submission was successful) placed both me and my writings under his rigorous and scholarly microscope and reflected back what he perceived to be the essential features of my life and work. Perhaps his most telling discovery was that, for 30 years, I have been nourished by two different communities of faith – that of person-centred practitioners and theoreticians and that of the Christian Church and its theologians. Lynch sketched out in his thesis some of the tensions as well as the frequent congeniality for me of my dual membership of these two communities. His biographical study also revealed that my membership of the Christian Church preceded by more than 20 years my entry into the world of person-centred therapy. For me the whole experience of being placed under the researcher's gaze was both humbling and illuminating; it is also relevant to the publication of this book.

This is the second time that I have had the privilege of bringing between the covers of a single volume a number of previously published – and some unpublished – chapters and papers. For the second time, too, I owe this opportunity to the generous invitation of Whurr Publishers and of series editor, Professor Windy Dryden. The first volume *Person-Centred Counselling: Therapeutic and Spiritual Dimensions* (1991) was, I recognise in retrospect, an undoubted publishing risk for it already gave clear evidence of the influence of the two communities of faith that Lynch's doctoral thesis examines. The danger was that the book would fall ignominiously between two stools and would be greeted by a deafening silence from members of both communities. The fact that it has now been reprinted five times and continues to be the generator of correspondence both to me and to professional journals suggests that my struggle to integrate my therapeutic work with my spiritual and religious life reflects the preoccupations of many of my fellow professionals and not a few of my

ix

co-religionists. The time is propitious, it would seem, for the dialogue (in my own mind and heart) sometimes harmonious, sometimes anguished, to be further conducted in the public arena.

In Chapter 9 of the present volume I argue that, in the past few years, it has become increasingly necessary for therapists of all persuasions to concern themselves with the spiritual dimension of experience and that there has been something of a sea-change in the attitude of many practitioners to this task. I believe this shift to be in many ways client-driven for it is now common for people to present themselves to therapists with concerns that they themselves have categorised as specifically spiritual in nature. There are, however, more profound issues at stake. In the face of the bewildering complexity of the manifold distress that clearly afflicts increasing numbers of end-of-century men and women, therapists, psychologists and many medical practitioners, too, are learning a new humility. There is a refreshing preparedness to turn to the wisdom of the ancient spiritual traditions and also to respect the integrity of those pioneers who have the courage to live at the cutting edge of spiritual awareness and to risk the ignominy of being branded as naive 'new agers'. The current predicament of humanity with the threat of ecological disaster and the apparent uncontrollability of rampant consumerism and electronic technology demands a passionate commitment to the search for spiritual enlightenment and direction that can only be served by the humility that acknowledges that the truth lies beyond all known psychologies, technologies, philosophies and theologies.

For some potential readers their acceptance of the spiritual and their willingness to engage with it are probably impeded by their experience of institutional religion with its alarming capacity for breeding intolerance and exacerbating inappropriate guilt. They will therefore regard with legitimate suspicion a therapist whose spirituality continues to find nourishment from the Christian tradition and who even maintains his membership of the much maligned Church of England. I know only too well that I risk loss of credibility at best and total rejection at worst both from those for whom Christianity has been the source of untold pain and misery and from those fellow Christians who will regard me as a liberal heretic doing Lucifer's work. I have no option, however, but to court such calumny. As a person-centred therapist I am committed to transparency and to the trusting of my own experience. As a Christian I am committed to a faith that has enabled me to know myself as infinitely beloved and inseparably joined to the source of all Love. I can only tell it as it is for me and trust that my readers will at least be persuaded of my integrity even if they cannot accompany me on my particular pilgrimage. It is my conviction that we will all meet in the absolute freedom of eternity and will recognise that we have never been parted from each other. But eternity is now if we did but know it. I suppose it is because, intermittently, I glimpse the awesomeness of such paradoxes that, as a

person-centred therapist, I have the audacity on rare occasions to do
what Carl Rogers himself gave up doing at an early age: I stand in a
pulpit and preach – but only, I hasten to add, when I have been warmly
invited to do so.

Brian Thorne
Norwich, 1997

PART I
Behold the Man[1]

Introduction

The publication in 1991 of *Behold the Man* by the religious publishers, Darton, Longman & Todd Limited, was for me a kind of watershed. Although up to that point I had not attempted to conceal my Christianity or my religious affiliations, I had been at pains in my professional writings to embrace the concept of spirituality while displaying considerable ambivalence (which I feel) towards religion. This had been a deliberate and conscious decision on my part because I wished to keep the lines of communication open with those whose stereotypical concept of religion let alone of the institutional Church would have made it impossible, I believed, for them to grant me any kind of hearing if they had known of my religious involvement. Once *Behold the Man* was in the public domain I knew that I had, as it were, finally blown my cover. The book was the direct outcome of my having stood in the pulpit of an Anglican church on Good Friday and could not possibly be understood as anything other than a profound expression of my commitment to the Christian faith and to the transformative power of the exemplar of human nature revealed in the life, death and resurrection of Jesus Christ.

Gordon Lynch in his doctoral thesis, referred to in the Prologue, more than hints that my perception of Jesus bears an uncanny resemblance to Carl Rogers' concept of the fully functioning person. Lynch draws attention to my insistence on Jesus' deep trust in the core of his own being and my demonstration of his empathy with and acceptance of those around him. He also makes much of my reflections on Jesus' birth

---

[1] *Behold the Man* was first published by Darton, Longman & Todd Ltd in 1991. It has subsequently been republished by IJA Publications (Bangalore) in 1997 and is currently being translated into French for publication in 1999. Extracts and themes from this book are also to be found in some of the sermons that form Part IV of this present volume.

1

and childhood (about which Scripture tells us very little) and sees this as further evidence of my desire to make Jesus fit a person-centred mould of human perfection. It is difficult to know how best to respond to this view for I cannot deny its apparent validity. For me, however, the telling and ultimately critical fact is that the Jesus whom I attempt to portray in *Behold the Man*, is the person I deeply encountered when I was a boy of nine and whom the Gospel of St John further reveals to my understanding. It is not a case of my moulding Jesus to fit person-centred personality theory but of person-centred theory further illuminating the nature of the Jesus whom I had known long since.

The response to *Behold the Man* was for me little short of astounding. Not only was it sympathetically reviewed in both Christian and psychotherapeutic journals but it released an avalanche of mail that assured me that there were many in both worlds who found in its pages inspiration and encouragement for their own spiritual and professional journeys. To receive letters of appreciation on the same day from a prominent psychoanalyst and an Australian contemplative monk convinced me that in future I need not perhaps be so coy about my spiritual and religious inheritance.

The book is now out of print in this country although an Indian edition has recently been published and a French translation is due to appear in 1998. It is therefore particularly pleasing to be able to include a substantial part of the text in this present volume.

Introduction

When my friend, David Clark, Rector of Oadby, invited me to give the addresses at the traditional Good Friday services in his parish, I felt both privileged and apprehensive. I sensed that such an undertaking would involve confronting the central doctrines of the Christian faith and I knew, too, that I would be standing in a pulpit on the day in the Christian year perhaps most charged with emotion.

My decision to accept the invitation was prompted by a number of seemingly unrelated factors. In the first place, the beginnings of my own Christian commitment stem from a profound experience that occurred on Good Friday 1946 when I was a boy of nine. For me the encounter with the suffering Christ on that day gave meaning to my life. Secondly, as a therapist I spend much of my life being a companion to those who are in pain and I could dimly sense the challenge of what it might involve to attempt to enter empathically into the sufferings of Jesus at the time of his greatest torment and into the minds of those caught up with him in the events leading to Calvary. Thirdly, I had in the previous three months read four books, all of which had made a profound impression on me and which tended to confirm many of my own discoveries along the path of Christian commitment. Gradually I began to realise that David Clark's invitation might enable me to articulate, within the rigorous framework of five brief addresses, at least some of my own deepest struggles as I attempt to be a Christian in the world of the late twentieth century. The books by Stephen Verney (*Water into Wine*), John Taylor (*Weep Not For Me*) Donald Allchin (*Participation in God*) and Jim Cotter (*Prayer at Night*) were my constant sources of encouragement and stimulation.[1] More than that, the very knowledge that four

---

[1] Stephen Verney (1985) *Water into Wine: An Introduction to John's Gospel.* London: Collins, Fount. John V Taylor (1986) *Weep Not For Me: Meditations on the Cross and the Resurrection.* Geneva: World Council of Churches. AM Allchin (1988) *Participation in God: A Forgotten Strand in the Anglican Tradition.* London: Darton, Longman & Todd. Jim Cotter (1983) (ed.) *Prayer at Night.* Liverpool: Cairns Publications

such priests exist within the ranks of the Church of England assures me that, despite much recent evidence to the contrary, my own beloved part of the Anglican Communion can still offer the kind of acceptance, understanding and openness that my soul requires for its proper nourishment. I hope these gifted men will forgive my plundering of their treasures.

The six meditations that follow (one has been added especially for this book) are based on the original addresses. My predominant reliance on St John's Gospel was almost inevitable after my reading of Stephen Verney's inspired introduction to its astonishing riches. The book concludes with an extended discussion of the personality of Jesus as revealed in the Passion narrative and its relevance to the work of a therapist.

Chapter 1
Corporate Betrayal

It was night. (John 13.30)[1]

As the climax of the Passion narrative approaches, the forces of darkness gather about Jesus with what seems like an inexorable momentum of their own. As Judas leaves the group and goes out into the night it seems that love is rendered powerless even at the most intimate level of friendship. It is, in fact, a terrible moment in the human drama. Judas has been in the company of Jesus for three years: he has experienced at close quarters the greatest love that the world has ever known and for much of that time we can only assume that he has responded to that love warmly and spontaneously. Certainly it would seem that he has worked hard for it is he who has been responsible for money management and for the distribution of alms. He was, one assumes, an intelligent man and the others must have held him in esteem. And now at this crucial time he goes out to hand over the Prince of Light to the Prince of Darkness. For some reason he can no longer respond to the love so freely offered and determines instead to work for its destruction.

In human relationships the story is only too common. Two people love each other and enter into a commitment. They promise to cherish and care for each other and to dedicate themselves to each other's well-being. And then after a while it all goes wrong. Boredom enters in, frustration, anger, jealousy or indifference. What began full of hope and the best of intentions ends in bitterness and separation. The same can happen between parents and children. Only a week or so ago I listened to the agony of a divorced mother whose only son had, without apparent reason, turned against her, left home and thrown up his place at college. For that woman it was night indeed. She cried out in her grief,

---

[1]Those readers wishing to follow the Passion narratives on which *Behold the Man* is based are referred to the Gospel of St John 13: 1–30; 18; 19: 1–30 (*New English Bible* translation).

'I love him so much and now he seems determined to punish me beyond endurance.'

Let us try to face the darkness. It is only too easy to protect ourselves from it by seeking security in our bourgeois culture or even by coming together in a holy huddle in church. Good Friday is not the time for such evasion. There is something of brutal realism in Christ's words when he said to the daughters of Jerusalem, 'Do not weep for me: weep for yourselves and for your children.' He commands us not to seek refuge in false emotion but to look at ourselves and at the world and not to flinch from the evidence of what we see. Judas, when he left the Upper Room, was rejecting love; indeed he went out in order to set in train a course of events that would lead to love being crucified on a cross. What is it in us that today leads to the same rejection and the same kind of murder? There is, of course, a number of glib answers possible. For Christians the typical response is to talk about original sin. This slippery and misunderstood doctrine has led many to think of human nature as corrupt or at best inclined to evil so that almost every example of human iniquity can be explained by the facile comment, 'it's human nature'. It's human nature to tell lies, to fiddle the income tax, to deceive one's partner, to beat the children, to ignore the starving, to lust for possessions, to reject the mentally ill, to harass the homosexual: ultimately it is human nature, by this analysis, to betray God with a kiss and to connive at his death on a cross. Judas, after all, was only being human.

In this and the subsequent meditations I want to challenge this concept of humanity and I want to do so by attempting imaginatively to come alongside Our Lord in the final hours of his life. I want us to participate in the Passion and Crucifixion by sharing in the mind of Jesus as he experiences what it means to be a man confronting his death. After all, Our Lord was only being human.

As Jesus sits at supper he is filled with unease: the very time when he is stretched to the utmost in the expression of his loving – the feet-washing, the symbolic enactment of self-giving in the blessing and sharing of the bread and the wine, the intimacy of the group of friends with the man he loved most resting against his breast – in the midst of all this Jesus is anxious. He senses betrayal. So great is his anxiety that he gives voice to it: 'Someone is going to hand me over; someone here: that will be terrible for me but for the person who does it will be even more terrible.' The others are appalled and break into loud protestations. John is incited to ask Jesus to be more specific but Jesus cannot bring himself to name Judas. Instead, he indicates him indirectly. But if we are to believe the account in John's gospel, John himself is left in no uncertainty; Jesus makes it clear to John that Judas is the person. Even if all the others remain confused, John knows. My hunch is that Peter did, too, and some of the others sitting close to Jesus.

If we believe that Jesus knew all along what was going to happen and if we believe that Judas was a mere puppet having to take his allotted role because this was part of the great plan laid down in Scripture, then I fear there can be no hope for us. This would mean that we are programmed, controlled, without freedom to grow or develop. It would also mean that we are quite beyond each other's reach, unable to choose intimacy or separation, closeness or distance, love or indifference.

As we attempt to enter the mind of Jesus as he and his disciples go out into the night I would suggest that we might be surprised at the confusion there. Undoubtedly he is in anguish about Judas. How can it be that so good a friend has turned against him? He will be longing for a change of heart in Judas: he will be consumed with a sense of the power-lessness of his own love to keep Judas in relationship with him. But as I try to enter the mind of Jesus I find myself stumbling upon another and unexpected feeling, which is somehow more disturbing. It is a sense of bewildered sadness at the behaviour of the beloved John and then by extension of all the others in the group. John, at Peter's request, had extracted from Jesus the identity of the betrayer. He knew, therefore, something of the enormity of what was about to happen. He certainly knew that Judas was not hurrying away to pay the bills. He did nothing – and the others did nothing. Not a word to Judas, not even the most feeble attempt to stop him, nobody to pursue him into the night to discover the source of his pain and bitterness. So Jesus leaves the Upper Room and goes out into the night, his heart breaking for Judas and weighed down with sorrow at the apparent indifference of the others to Judas's plight. It was as if they had been paralysed by the apparent powerlessness of his own love: if Jesus could not keep Judas within their company what hope had they? For Jesus, I suggest, it must have felt very different. Why was it, he must have asked himself, that nobody, not even John whom he loved so dearly, had been able to say to Judas: 'We love you, you are one of us: where are you going? what are you intending to do?' Why was it that not one of them had seen that Jesus' impotent love needed the expression of theirs to regain its power? Why had they not been able to see that being truly human is impossible on your own?

Chapter 2
Jesus and the Evil of Religion

'We have a law; and by that law he ought to die.' (John 19:7)

It is never easy for those of us who belong to a religious group – and especially perhaps for those of us who are members of a State church – to face the shocking truth that Jesus went to his death hated and condemned by the religious leaders of his day. What is more, they planned and plotted and stirred up their followers in order to achieve his downfall. Theirs was a deliberate, premeditated and passionately implemented campaign of destruction. And they did it in the name of the God of Israel and in order to uphold the sacred Law. They saw themselves and were seen by others as virtuous men, upholders of the faith and the protectors of the holy tradition. To see them as political schemers, more interested in humiliating Pilate than in having Jesus put to death is, I believe, to evade the full impact of the appalling truth – that virtuous God-fearing men can become murderers precisely because of their virtue and their God-fearing disposition. Not, of course, that one should be surprised by this. After all the history of Christendom down to our own times is packed full of examples of the same grim phenomenon. Perhaps in our own day holy Christian men connive at character assassination rather than literal murder and we should be grateful for this marginal improvement. Certainly, however, they continue to use the holy Law as found in Scripture as the blunt instrument with which to assault their loving but disturbing victims. 'We have a law and by our law he ought to be defrocked and hounded out of office.'

Jesus, we must remember, loved his people and was steeped in the traditions of his forefathers. By many he was himself perceived as a rabbi, a teacher of the Law. Throughout his life, as far as we know, he worshipped in the synagogue and preached there. When he was aged 12, he was to be found in the great Temple at Jerusalem among the priests and scholars, debating with them and asking them questions. In the days before his arrest he was once more in the Temple addressing the crowds. We need to remember all this as we attempt to enter the mind of Jesus as he watches the crowd approaching him in the garden, Judas at the head with the lanterns illuminating their weapons. Here is his friend of yesterday leading a band of people many of whom Jesus must have known well from his many hours spent in the Temple. He must often have chatted with the Temple guards and the other Temple officials. Malchus, the unfortunate servant who was to lose an ear, albeit temporarily, was probably well known to him. This, then, was not a band of strangers: they were his co-religionists, some of whom he would have instantly recognised. John's account of the meeting in the garden is extraordinary on several counts but chiefly because it suggests that Jesus was by now calm within himself. The agitation in the Upper Room and the agony of the prayer to the Father are replaced by a loving sadness that is all-pervasive. We are told that the band of soldiers and officials is momentarily stopped in its tracks as Jesus comforts Malchus and heals his ear. He is, it seems, in command of himself and radiates love and power. But – and it is an enormous 'but' – this power that can heal and dazzle is in other ways without strength. Jesus does not or cannot resist arrest and the men who have come to seize him continue in their task despite the evidence that they have themselves witnessed of his radiance and healing power. Jesus, in short, endures once again the experience of the impotence of his own loving. He is self-possessed, full of light and compassion and yet faced with the implacable force of religious zeal and hatred he is powerless to resist. The precise moment of the encounter is worth reflecting on in detail.

> Jesus went out to them and asked,
> 'Who is it you want?'
> 'Jesus of Nazareth,' they answered. Jesus said,
> 'I am he.'

And there stood Judas, the traitor, with them. When he said, 'I am he', they stood back and fell to the ground. Again Jesus asked, 'Who is it you want?' 'Jesus of Nazareth,' they answered. Then Jesus said, 'I have told you that I am he.'

These two bold utterances of Jesus 'I am he' confirm the striking picture of a man who is completely at home in his own identity. He is being fully himself – loving, healing, inwardly strong and composed. And yet a few moments later he is in bonds and is led away, an apparently helpless prisoner. People who are so firmly at home in their own skin are always impressive. They stand out from the crowd because they are not dependent on others for their own sense of self-worth. They are free to think their own thoughts, own their own feelings and express what they experience without giving way to their own fear of psychological or physical attack. It is clear that Jesus is impressive in this way and it is for this reason that, momentarily, the soldiers and officials are literally bowled over by his presence. They cannot bear a person who is so fully and assuredly himself. A moment's thought reveals to us that it is precisely the individual who is secure in his own identity, the person who with confidence can say, 'I am', that many religions find so threatening. Indeed, it seems to be the particular talent of certain religious people to ensure that individuals can never develop such a sense of strength in their own identity. The weapon they choose is that of condemnation, which in turn induces a deep sense of guilt in the victim so that he goes through life a psychological cripple unable to affirm the beauty and wonder of his own nature.

I recall some 11 years ago, at an international conference in Paris, convening an impromptu seminar for those who wished to explore the relationship between psychological and spiritual development and how, within half an hour of the start, almost the whole group was in tears as one member after another talked about his or her experiences at the hands of the churches – both Catholic and Protestant. I still remember some of the stories now. There was the man brought up in a Catholic boarding school where the staff – mostly priests – inflicted a vicious round of humiliating punishments for the smallest misdemeanours and seemed to derive sadistic satisfaction from inflicting corporal punishment on lonely and frightened young adolescents. There was the woman who had had her mouth washed out with soap by a nun for saying the equivalent of 'shit' and then been made to stand barefoot in the chapel for an hour without moving. There was the account of a Calvinist minister who had told a fifteen year-old that she was possessed by the devil and should on no account enter a chapel building. The stories were not only of priests, nuns and ministers but also of parents whose religious beliefs and practices seemed to make it impossible for them to relate to their children without at the same time judging them, condemning them and making them feel so burdened with guilt that life was almost intolerable. For me that impromptu seminar was saved from turning into a complete nightmare by the contribution of a Swiss woman who told how, as an adolescent, she, too, had felt utterly guilty, unable to find any virtue in herself and totally despairing. In her distress she had rung the bell of a house of the Jesuit fathers and had collapsed sobbing into the arms of the priest who opened the door to her. Strangely enough he did not welcome her in but instead himself left the house and taking her arm walked for two hours with her in a nearby park. At the end of that time, she said, her despair had lifted and for the first time for years she felt that she had value. It was only some years later that she discovered that the priest who had walked in the park with her was Fr Pierre Teilhard de Chardin. It is perhaps not without its significance that de Chardin himself, brilliant scientist and mystic, was later to prove too tiresome for the Jesuit order and the Catholic Church and was severely censured. His mind and heart were too free to be shackled by the bonds of so-called orthodoxy. For the moment I need to pause and reflect with great sadness on those countless individuals over the years who have come to seek my help because they were so loaded with guilt that life had become well-nigh impossible. None of those people, as I recall it, had done anything particularly appalling – there were no murderers or rapists, arsonists or swindlers. A guilt that was elusive but all pervading afflicted them, a sense of being in the wrong, of never being able to please those whose love they craved, of being eternally without value.

As Jesus stands before Annas – and again we should not assume that the two men were strangers to each other (we are told, for example, that one of the disciples at least was an acquaintance of Annas) – he remains impervious to the condemnation and no sense of guilt assails him. On the contrary, Jesus speaks firmly, almost provocatively. 'Why do you question me?' he asks. 'I taught openly in the Temple. If you want to know what I said, ask them who listened to me.' For this defiant remark he receives a blow in the face from one of the men guarding him and is accused of gross insolence. Again he does not flinch or capitulate. He does not accept the accusation and he refuses to feel guilty. Instead he replies, 'If I spoke amiss, state it in evidence against me: if I spoke well why do you hit me?'

Here, then, we see once more a man who is utterly secure in his own identity and who cannot be touched at the core of his being by the false accusations of the religious leaders. And, of course, they are infuriated. To their followers they portray Jesus as the blasphemer, the threat to national honour and to the faith of their forefathers. It is likely, too, that Annas, Caiaphas and the other chief priests genuinely saw it as their responsibility to preserve the Jewish nation and the Jewish faith. At a deeper level, however, we see the insidious workings of the lust for power and the egocentric craving to retain personal power and to preserve the absolute authority of the ecclesiastical institution. That is why religion can be a most destructive force in the life of human souls: it lends itself to an unscrupulous authoritarianism which cannot bear the uniqueness of persons and which beneath a cloak of virtue seeks to destroy those who by their inner security threaten its domination. As Jesus stands before Annas and then before Caiaphas he suffers the depth of anguish which comes from being truly himself only to discover that in doing so he is despised, condemned and rejected by those who profess to serve the same God that resides in his own heart. But Jesus does not succumb: he admits no guilt, he refuses to accept the judgement, his light reveals the darkness of his accusers. He is the great 'I am' and his identity remains unshaken even in the midst of the most intense internal suffering. Not all can be so resolute: in another part of the courtyard, Peter is busily saying, 'I am not'.

Chapter 3
Jesus and Political Power

'You are not Caesar's friend.' (John 19:12)

Perhaps, like me, you have always had some sneaking sympathy for Pontius Pilate. I imagine him as a man who never fulfilled his ambitions as a Roman administrator. His appointment as Prefect of Judea in AD26 was not exactly a plum job and one can only imagine that Pilate hoped it would be short term and would lead to greater things. In fact he remained in office for 10 years, the second longest holder of the prefect-ship. If we are to believe the historical writings of Philo Judaeus and Flavius Josephus it seems that Pilate was a blundering, insensitive and often brutal fellow who was keen to show his loyalty to the Emperor by some manifestation of devotion to the imperial service. It is recorded that on one occasion he allowed Roman troops to bring their military standards into Jerusalem with the busts of the Emperor, which were, of course, considered idolatrous images by the Jews. What is more, he did it in an underhand manner and had the troops bring in and set up the images by night. The Jews orchestrated a massive sit-down and lie-down protest demonstration and Pilate had to back down. On another occasion it seems the Jews sent letters of protest to Rome about Pilate's behaviour and the Emperor himself intervened to make Pilate remove golden shields with the Emperor's own name on them that he had placed in his residence in Jerusalem. In short, then, Pilate, it seems, had a knack of doing things guaranteed to infuriate the Jews and thus lead to civil disturbances, which in turn would earn him a black mark in the Emperor's book.

When the chief priests accused him of not being Caesar's friend they knew they were hitting at a particularly tender spot. It was, in fact, a scarcely veiled threat. They were as good as saying, 'If you don't put this man to death we shall be reporting you to Rome and we shall tell the Emperor that you took no action against someone who is not only a blasphemer in our eyes but a direct threat to the Emperor's own rule.'

Poor Pilate! He so wanted the Emperor's approval and once again he was threatened with a situation that could lead to his censure and possible recall to Rome in disgrace.

It is in the light of all this that I continue to feel my sneaking sympathy for Pilate. After all, he did make some effort to avoid committing Jesus to death. There can be little doubt that he believed Jesus innocent and had no wish to see him crucified. One of the Gospels (Matthew) records that his wife, by tradition a lady called Procla, had a message sent to him while he was with Jesus imploring him to be careful because she had had a disturbing dream about Jesus that previous night. Such a message must have weighed on him profoundly and made him all the more concerned to spare Jesus if he could. Pilate wriggles and squirms in order not to become Jesus' executioner: he pleads Jesus' innocence before the crowd; he offers them Jesus as the traditional prisoner to be released at the Passover; he symbolically washes his hands to try to be rid of the responsibility. But then, in the dismal words of John, 'At last to satisfy them, he handed over Jesus to be crucified.'

As we attempt to enter the mind of Jesus as he stands before Pilate we are caught up in the history of nations. Jesus the Jew confronts the representative of the occupying forces. Pilate, the Roman patrician, faces a man brought to him as a criminal by the leaders of a subjugated people. It is a meeting between the man at the top of the political pyramid and a troublemaker from the mob. And yet the remarkable fact is that Pilate has no power at all to disturb the inner equilibrium of Jesus. In fact it is Pilate who is forced by his role into complete inauthenticity. For Jesus there is once again the experience of calmness and apparent powerlessness. In the garden he has been faced by the forces of religious zeal and hatred – now he is faced by political power and the result is the same. Just as the band in the garden had recognised Jesus' radiance but had gone on to arrest him, so Pilate recognises Jesus' innocence but goes on to condemn him.

Jesus, it is clear, tries to communicate to Pilate. He tackles him on the source of the idea that he is a king but Pilate is merely angry and seems insulted as if he is being accused of being a Jew himself. His racial prejudice is such that he cannot engage with Jesus in rational discourse. The climax of their meeting is reached when Jesus states that his task is to bear witness to the truth and Pilate replies in the words which have made him infamous down the centuries: 'What is truth?' Jesus suffers the agony of sensing the man behind the politician and not being able to reach him. Pilate for his part is hopelessly caught. He recognises the innocence of Jesus but his fear and hatred of the Jews make it impossible for him to act on his perception. More than that he is also the prisoner of his own cynicism. His question 'What is truth?' is the cynical comment of a man who has come to live a life ruled by political expediency and by the fear of forfeiting power. Truth is the last thing with which he can be concerned; he has instead to think of what will please the Emperor and preserve his own skin and position. The dialogue is an amazing one. It is not Jesus who is troubled in spirit. He speaks directly and unambiguously and is then flogged and repeatedly humiliated. But he retains his inner strength and is prepared to maintain silence as Pilate seeks to question him further. He even has the compassion to focus on Pilate's mounting guilt feelings and to speak words of comfort: 'The deeper guilt lies with the man who handed me over to you.' No, it is not Jesus who is troubled but Pilate who is thrown more and more into confusion and agony of mind. No wonder, for he it is who becomes the channel for the corporate evil of the whole society gathered in Jerusalem at that time. There is no chance, it seems, for Pontius Pilate to be the person he had it in him to become: he has relinquished his personhood in the pursuit of power and worldly ambition so that, faced by the pure humanity of Jesus, he can recognise it but not protect it. This is a meeting between a fully developed human being and a man who has squandered his humanity in the hunt for power. When Pilate eventually hands Jesus over he knows that he has lost the power struggle on all fronts. He has capitulated to the Jews and in the presence of the Man he has failed to be anything more than a pathetic provincial administrator who cannot even heed the promptings of his wife's unconscious.

How often does Jesus meet with Pilate in our day? In our own nation's life it would seem that it is becoming more and more difficult for politicians and administrators to avoid becoming, like Pilate, the channels for the corporate evil working in the institutions of the cosmos. Is the DSS official behind his plate glass window able to respond as a person to the distraught young mother whose cheque has not come through? Is the Cabinet minister able to hear the cry of the prisoners whose major crime is to have fallen victim to the materialistic affluence that he has worked to create? As Our Lord spoke with Pilate in the year AD 33, he represented for all time the struggle of the individual human being to affirm the unique value of the person in the face of those who have surrendered their humanity to political ideology and the pursuit of power.

> Pilate said to the Jews, 'Here is your King.' They shouted, 'Away with him! Away with him! Crucify him!'
> 'Crucify your King?' said Pilate. 'We have no king but Caesar', the Jews replied. Then at last, to satisfy them, he handed Jesus over to be crucified.

Chapter 4
Jesus and Those under Authority

'That is what the soldiers did.' (John 19:24)

Roman soldiers were disciplined men. Those who accompanied Jesus on the fateful walk to Golgotha had probably accompanied many convicted criminals before him. It was their job and it may seem unlikely that they would waste much thought or emotion wondering about the nature of the young rabbi whose inflammatory words and behaviour had earned him the death sentence. It was simply their task to carry out the most gruesome form of punishment known to the Roman Empire. Perhaps there was some sadistic pleasure in it but it is more likely that they felt demeaned by such sordid duties and longed for a more virile and admirable way of exercising their profession.

For Jesus himself the soldiers must have been a potent sign of the certainty of his destruction. They were themselves the powerless agents of superior authority and for them it would have been unthinkable to do anything other than carry out their orders. Not to have pushed him along the streets, not to have stripped him naked, not to have nailed him to the cross, not to have lifted that cross into its vertical position so that everyone could mock and gloat – not to have done any of these things would have been to fail in their duty and to court disgrace and probably their own execution. They were under orders and they had no option. In a sense, then, Jesus must have felt a strange sort of comradeship with his Roman captors for they were all caught in the same apparent trap. But there was a crucial difference: he was accepting of his journey towards death whereas they had no option but to accompany him upon that journey.

Perhaps the role of a soldier engaged in internal security duties is about as gross an affront to personal authenticity as can be imagined. I recall my own experience as a national serviceman in Cyprus many years ago when, as a young man, I found myself caught up in the struggle of EOKA terrorists to shake off the domination of the British colonial

15

authorities. During one particularly absurd week I found myself guard commander of a centre for women detainees who were suspected of being messengers or gunrunners for the terrorists. I was just 20 and my platoon were mostly teenagers from rural Gloucestershire; the detainees were almost all young Greek Cypriot women from high school. Emotionally the situation was an impossible one. In other circumstances the young men and women would have delighted in each others' company but in this grotesque situation the soldiers could have no contact with the women except that required by the ritual of the detention orders. One evening something inside me suddenly snapped. I suppose I could sense the onset of the internal desolation that always overwhelms me when I feel that I am about to lose hold of the core of my own identity. Whatever the reason I managed to engineer an hour when all the soldiers were occupied in various duties and I could talk furtively to the detainees not as the guard commander but as a person. They proved to me what I already knew. They were, in fact, the free ones and I was the prisoner. In their helplessness and vulnerability they were being true to themselves and their lives had meaning whereas I was the pawn of political and military forces that I could not control and that threatened to rob me of my identity. It is not for this realisation, however, that I chiefly recall that hour of intense and intimate conversation through the bars of police cell windows. It is rather for their loving response to me in that bizarre context that I shall always remember those young Greek Cypriot women. In their own powerlessness they were able to recognise that I was in the more appalling trap and they responded to my need. They gave me back a sense of my own dignity as a person and freed me from the shame of the role that I was compelled to enact.

I have no doubt that the loving understanding of unknown Greek Cypriot women towards a callow British second lieutenant is but a pale shadow of the feelings of the suffering Jesus towards the Roman soldiers who crucified him and tossed a coin for his tunic. Jesus throughout his life saw beyond the superficial appearances of those he encountered and he was always particularly drawn to those who seemed to have no power of their own. I am persuaded that in his heart he yearned to make contact with the persons hidden beneath the military uniforms and demeaned by the brutal behaviour which they were forced to inflict upon him. His surrendering of himself to them without resistance or struggle is a sign of his refusal to be anything but totally vulnerable and it is in vulnerability that love often makes itself most strikingly apparent. As he is nailed to the cross, the heart of Jesus overflows in sorrowing love for those whose humanity has been so monstrously aggressed that they have no option but to carry out a legalised murder. The naked and utterly defenceless man cries out in agony not only because of intolerable physical pain but out of love for all those whose lives are in thrall to any authority that is blind to the wonder and fragility of human nature.

St John tells us that there are four soldiers whose duty it was to crucify Jesus and we can imagine that each had his particular responsibility. Perhaps one would have stripped Jesus while another held him down and the others hammered in the nails. It is, of course, an astonishingly intimate form of execution. Flesh touches flesh repeatedly and blood spurts everywhere. For Jesus there is the overwhelming proximity of the soldiers whose bodies were presumably young, athletic and full of animal vigour. In the normal course of events they might well have rejoiced in each other's energy and found pleasure in each other's company despite the difference of race and culture. As it is, the initiative lies with the man who is psychologically free. We can never know how Jesus communicated his love and understanding to the soldiers who carried out his death sentence but it would seem that he can have done so only through the expressiveness of his tortured body. Flesh and blood are themselves the channels of love that communicate through the eyes of a dying man as he looks upon those under a dark authority and gives them back their humanity. A few hours later the centurion in charge of the crucifixion will bear witness to the fact that the love of Jesus has indeed broken through and irradiated the horrific climax of a sequence of events brought about by blind and corrupt power. 'Truly this was a son of God', he shouts, and his words attest to the fact that love has penetrated the role of the man under orders and reached to the heart of a person who longs to be as free as the victim whose cruel death he has dutifully supervised.

Chapter 5
Jesus and Women

'Near the cross where Jesus hung stood his mother, with her sister, Mary, wife of Clopas, and Mary of Magdala.' (John 19:25)

In my previous meditations I have tried to look at the power of political forces in order to understand their immense contribution to the crucifixion of Jesus. In some ways such reflections can keep us safely caught up in our intellects. They sanitise horror and make of it a subject for debate. It is like discussing the theology of apartheid rather than sharing imaginatively in the daily sufferings of an oppressed and humiliated people. But now the time has come to speak plainly of the brutality, hostility and hate in the Passion story. As John Taylor has shown so vividly, there is an unspeakable build-up of aggression and abuse as one group after another pile their hatred onto the defenceless body of this good man. It all seems so inexplicable. Why should so much violence have been discharged upon this man of all men? Why Judas's villainy, the man trusted with the common purse? Why should the teachers of the moral law, the Pharisees with their tremendous zeal for spiritual revival, be so set on getting rid of the young rabbi? Why were the high priests so utterly determined to drive the luckless Pilate to impose the sentence of death? Why did the guards in Caiaphas' hall suddenly start beating their prisoner about the head? Why did the normally well-disciplined Roman soldiers turn against their semi-conscious victim with another vicious burst of bullying? John Taylor suggests that, if we are honest, these questions are as unanswerable now as they were then. Somewhere in the world right now it is almost certain that guards, police or interrogators are viciously savaging an innocent victim. What is more, it is the innocent person who remains in control of himself who provokes the greatest rage in his oppressors. It is as if the torturers dimly realise that they are the ones without strength and the realisation is intolerable. The greater the light, it seems, the greater the darkness. The more calm and centred the innocence, the more the extreme brutality. It is as if total goodness is an affront that must be destroyed.

18

The Christ who hung on the cross, then, had been brutalised to a horrible degree. He was not even capable of carrying the cross-beam of his tree of execution and the passing Simon is coerced into service on the way to Calvary.

Mother Julian of Norwich does not shrink from telling us of the vision she had of the dying Jesus on the cross. The figure she sees is very far removed from the stylised image familiar to us from many a crucifix with its seemly loincloth and neatly contained wounds. This medieval mystic, much beloved in the city where I live, faced the full horror of the long drawn-out dying of a naked man who had been most viciously abused before he was even nailed to the cross.

> That blessed flesh and frame was drained of all blood and moisture. Because of the pull of the nails and the weight of that blessed body it was a long time suffering. For I could see that the great, hard, hurtful nails in those dear and tender hands and feet caused the wounds to gape wide and the body to sag forward under its own weight, and because of the time it hung there. His head was scarred and torn, and the crown was sticking to it, congealed with blood; his dear hair and his withered flesh was entangled with the thorns, and they with it. At first, when the flesh was still fresh and bleeding the constant pressure of the thorns made the wounds even deeper. Furthermore, I could see that the dear skin and tender flesh, the hair and the blood, were hanging loose from the bone, gouged by the thorns in many places. It seemed about to drop off, heavy and loose, still holding its natural moisture, sagging like a cloth. The sight caused me dreadful and great grief; I would have died rather than see it fall off. What the cause of it was I could not see, but I assumed that it was due to the sharp thorns, and the rough and cruel way the garland was pressed home heartlessly and pitilessly.[1]

In this way a medieval woman beheld her Lord as he hung dying on the first Good Friday. So it was, we may imagine, that on that day the four women closest to the cross beheld the suffering Jesus. Three were members of his family including his mother, Mary, the fourth is the woman we know as Mary Magdalen – healed of mental illness by Jesus and certainly one who loved him profoundly and who was later to be the privileged person who first encountered the Risen Lord. These women display great courage in showing their love to the dying man despite the mockery and jeers of the crowd and they show what seems to be an absolute fearlessness in the presence of the deepest suffering. Among the men only John, it seems, shows equal courage and fearlessness.

---

[1] Julian of Norwich, trans. Clifton Wolters (1966) *Revelations of Divine Love*. London: Penguin 1966, pp 88–9.

The life of Jesus is rich with stories of his encounters with women and it seems somehow appropriate that he should die supported by the loving presence of women after most of the men had turned tail and fled. As we remember his moving and intimate conversations with his mother, with Mary and Martha from Bethany, with the Samaritan woman at the well, with the woman with an issue of blood, with Jairus' daughter, with the widow of Nain, with the woman caught in adultery, it comes as no surprise to learn that Jesus was much loved by women. On the way to Golgotha we are told by Luke that great numbers of people followed, many women among them, who mourned and lamented over him. Against the stark brutality inflicted by the religious, political and military men, the women symbolise the beginnings of compassion and under-standing. Procla's dream-life reveals Jesus's innocence and the women of Jerusalem weep for the man they pity. On the way to the cross there is the beautiful tradition of Veronica who hands Jesus a napkin to wipe his bleeding face, which is then forever imprinted on the fabric. At the foot of the cross the four women wait in sorrow and love.

It is strange how often the role of women in the final hours of Jesus' life is either overlooked entirely or given scant attention. It is as if the many male commentators on the Passion and Crucifixion are somehow loath to acknowledge that without the women there would be scarcely a redeeming feature in the whole grim story of brutality, viciousness and hate. What, one wonders, would have been in the mind of Jesus as he experienced this female presence during his hours of greatest anguish?

I can only imagine that he must have experienced a profound sense of being loved in the midst of the most unspeakable agony. He is utterly powerless, stripped, grievously wounded, a terrible sight to behold. And yet the women are there – as Julian many hundreds of years later was to be there in her vision – fully conscious of the horror and the overwhelming pain but full of love for the man who had changed their lives. It is indeed remarkable that for so much of its history the Church has been dominated by a concept of woman as Eve, the temptress – somehow unreliable and dangerous in her loving. But in his last hours Jesus is loved and supported by women whose love is faithful and fearless to the end. Jesus on the cross experiences the love of women as capable of taking on the cosmic forces of darkness. Here are the lovers who are truly fitting companions for love incarnate in the hour of his deepest torment and despair. The daughters of Eve become the lovers of Christ and the crucified Lord knows their presence as the hour of death approaches. Who is this nailed on a cross who seems to have earned the hate and hostility of the patriarchal world of religion and politics but for whom women weep in distress and love? Who is this man who loved the adulteress and the prostitute? Who is this God from whom men flee and to whom women give their love without fear?

Chapter 6
The Divinisation of Humanity

'It is accomplished!' (John 19:30)

As the death of Jesus draws nearer minute by minute so our task of trying to enter his mind and spirit becomes increasingly difficult. We last thought of him caught in the gaze of women who love him. We have shared his pain and bewilderment at the treachery of Judas and the apparent paralysis of the other men who had been his intimates for three years. We have entered his inner calm and witnessed his self-control as he is confronted by the frustrated fury of religious and political leaders. We have perhaps dared to imagine something of the unbearable physical pain and anguish as he has endured the appalling assaults, beatings and the final brutality of the most obscene and humiliating punishment known to the Roman Empire.

Now, however, we are challenged at the deepest level by the mysteriousness of his extraordinary personality. His recorded words from the cross weave a bewildering pattern of despair and inner strength, of physical agony and astonishing detachment. As they are reported in the Gospels, we hear:

Father, forgive them, for they do not know what they are doing.

Eli, Eli lama sabachthani: my God, my God, why hast thou forsaken me?

I tell you this: today you shall be with me in Paradise.

Mother, there is your son.

Son, there is your mother.

I thirst.

Father into thy hands I commit my spirit.

It is accomplished.

What are we to make of these utterances from the lips of a dying man? I would suggest that we can discover in them the agony and the ecstacy of what it means to be fully human. Here we see before our eyes and hear ringing in our ears what it truly means to be a human being. In the first place, Jesus is open to the full range of existential torment. He knows what it means to feel utterly desperate, abandoned by the God in whom he had placed his complete trust. He knows what it means to grasp the hope which lies beyond despair and to trust again against all reason. Secondly, he knows what it is to be open to relationship at every level. He receives the love and respect of the condemned thief and responds in fullest measure without the least trace of judgement or withholding. He is loved and hated with intensity. To the hatred he responds with complete forgiveness; to the love he responds with an outpouring of his own love, which it seems we cannot even begin to understand. But to understand is our task if we are to enter into the mind and heart of Jesus. Let us, then, try once more to be with the dying Lord.

He sees through the blood and sweat of his agony and in the semi-consciousness of his dying hours, his mother – a middle-aged peasant woman who loves him passionately but who has let him go – and his dearest friend, probably a young man from a different class and of superior intellect. Both, he knows, will experience his death as the most appalling tragedy and their lives will be shattered. Jesus loves them with an intensity that transcends his agony. He joins them together, these two so different people, and we are told 'from that moment the disciple took her into his home'. Of course, this may simply mean that John gave Mary a place to live in and some security in her desolation but I am persuaded with Stephen Verney that it means very much more than this. Jesus is asking his mother and his dearest friend to enter into each other's hearts, to establish the deepest bonds of intimacy. He is asking them to overcome differences of age and sex, of background and intellect, and to be for each other as he has been for them. In short, he is inviting them to enter into a new reality of love that heralds a new age. This is what Jesus thirsts for and he thirsts for it in his physical anguish, in the body which is now dried up and parched, and in his spirit which yearns that we may find unity in our uniqueness and diversity.

When those final words come from his lips, 'it is accomplished', we hear the proclamation that a human person has achieved the fullness of being. This is what is possible when a human being dares to be fully himself.

How supremely difficult it is for us to identify with the dying Jesus. To enter his mind and heart is to move into a world of mystery and paradox – of despair and hope, of naked and suffering flesh and of agonising yet finally triumphant spirit, of the intensity of love both received and given. Perhaps in some ways it is easier to be with the beloved disciple, John. He, remember, only a few hours previously had been powerless to stretch out to the treacherous Judas, but now he is at the foot of the cross, the only man who dares to give expression to his love and tenderness. What is more he responds to the request of the dying Jesus to find room in his heart for Mary and in so doing he demonstrates the kind of loving which he has himself received from his dying friend. Age, sex, background, intellect are no barrier: they melt away as love flows from the dying Jesus in the way that soon blood and water will flow from his dead and mutilated body.

Perhaps it is easier to identify with John because John is, as it were, one of us – a real human being, not a mysterious Christ. In the same way we can perhaps dimly imagine the experience of Mary Magdalen on the first Easter morning as she blinks through her tears and sees the gardener. She, too, seems reassuringly human. But I am going to insist: our task is to dare to be with Jesus.

Let us go back to an earlier time when he was in danger of being stoned by the Jews. Listen.

> Once again the Jews picked up stones to stone him. At this Jesus said to them, 'I have set before you many good deeds, done by my Father's power; for which of these would you stone me?' The Jews replied, 'We are not going to stone you for any good deed, but for your blasphemy. You, a mere man, claim to be a god.' Jesus answered, 'Is it not written in your Law, "I said: You are gods?" Those are called gods to whom the word of God was delivered . . .Then why do you charge me with blasphemy because I, consecrated and sent into the world by the Father said, "I am God's son?"'[1]

Here, then, is the awesome key that can begin to set us free to come alongside the dying Lord. The truth is that we find it so difficult to identify with Jesus because we are not reconciled to the mysteriousness of our own natures. We will not or cannot, it seems, accept what the Psalmist says in the very passage that Jesus uses to defend himself from the charge of blasphemy: 'We are gods yet we shall die like men.' We flee from the awesome, unbelievable truth that to be fully human is to share in the divine nature and that is why we want to distance ourselves from the dying Christ as if he is not really one of us at all. But he is and he is the Son of God, as we are children of God. As our beloved friend he dies to show us what it means to accept our true natures. The cry 'it is accomplished' is the proclamation of the New Age that dawned on the first Good Friday. It tells us that God became man so that man might become God. These are the words of Athanasius, so brilliantly illuminated by Donald Allchin in his 1988 book *Participation in God*. As our dear Lord

---

[1]John 10:31–42

dies on the cross, if we are truly prepared to be with him we have no option but to recognise ourselves for the first time and to grasp what it means to be truly human. We are called to participate in the divine nature and to be taken into a relationship of complete intimacy with God. But Jesus could not do it on his own and nor can we. He needed the love of his Father but when he could no longer feel that love he rested in the love of women and the love of a man who had overcome fear and was free from the bonds of religious bigotry and political power games. In the end, it is not the mysteriousness of Jesus that is the stumbling block. It is the blinding clarity with which his death demonstrates to us the divine quality of our own natures and the fearlessness of the loving we need from each other if we are to be fully human. 'Behold the man', said Pilate – and in that statement he gave the answer to his own cynical question 'What is truth?' The truth is within each one of us and what happened on Calvary challenges us to see it and not to be afraid. With such a vision and with such fearlessness we shall recognise that we are members one of another and we shall live in a new created world.

Chapter 7
A Therapist's View of the Passion Narrative

The Jesus whom we have accompanied through the appalling sufferings of the Passion narrative is at all times firmly in touch with the centre of his own being. If it were not so he would rapidly have been overwhelmed by events and would have ended as no more than a pathetic and misunderstood prophet, executed by the Romans because they had been persuaded that he was a political threat. Jesus, however, is not overwhelmed. It is true that he is rendered completely powerless and stripped of every vestige of human dignity, but in the deepest recesses of his being he remains firmly in touch with his own authority. Even on the cross he is able to call up reserves of love and compassion which enable him to respond to his mother and friend and even, I have suggested, to those responsible for carrying out his execution. In short, he remains true to himself in the midst of the most savage assaults on his identity.

The preceding paragraph is, of course, a therapist's psychological interpretation of events. A biblical scholar might express things differently. He might point to the relationship that Jesus has with his Father and see him as delivering himself up into the hands of the Father, a process which only momentarily founders when he cries out in dereliction from the cross and seems to experience utter abandonment. On this understanding of events Jesus is sustained through his suffering not by his ability to stay in touch with himself but by his utter dependence on the will and support of God, the Father.

It can be argued, and indeed has been, that the two interpretations amount to the same thing. Christopher Bryant, for example, writing of St Augustine's famous dictum, 'O God, thou has made us for thyself and our hearts are restless until they rest in thee', has this to say:

> But if we understand the desire of God as the desire to be at one with our true centre, the desire to live in accordance with the truth of our being, then this ancient doctrine is infused with new

and exciting meaning. The desire to rest in God will be seen as a
desire to live from our centre, to express our own truth, to be
centred, integrated, a city at unity in itself.[1]

Bryant is here pointing to the concept of God within, a loving presence
residing in the very heart of the individual that becomes indistinguish-
able from the person's deepest sense of identity. Creator and creature
become united in the same substance.

For the therapist it is a daily experience to meet people who have no
sense of their own identity and who endure life as fragmented beings
with no awareness of the glory of being human. On the contrary they are
customarily without worth in their own eyes and feel themselves to be
unlovable. Not infrequently they are weighed down with shame at their
own inability to relate to others and their total lack of trust that others
will treat them with respect. It is the therapist's task – often conducted
over many years and with many false starts and cul-de-sacs – to bring
such people to an awareness of their own identity and to a trust in their
essential value and goodness. The obstacles in the way of such a
pilgrimage (for it is a spiritual journey) are formidable and in the Passion
narrative they are illuminated with a chilling starkness.

The betrayal of Judas points to the fickleness of friendship and to the
inability of even a close-knit group to respond to its individual members
with love and understanding. And yet no human being can be human on
his own and when Judas is left alone in his treachery there is nothing
that can impede his descent into darkness. The disciples, as they sat at
supper on the first Maundy Thursday, resemble many a family or friendship group where patterns of relationship contrive to produce a scapegoat usually through jealousy, envy or resentment. Judas, it seems, is
made the receptacle for all the negative feelings in the group (for which
of the disciples could have been totally free of anger against Jesus for
having brought them into such danger and confusion?). It is Judas,
therefore, who becomes the betrayer and sets out to destroy the love
from which he now feels alienated.

Jesus himself emerges from the Upper Room deeply wounded by
Judas and accompanied by those who will soon forsake him in the same
way that they have abandoned Judas to his fate. Whereas Judas will later
kill himself, however, Jesus will not fall victim to self-rejection. He will
survive the emotional bludgeoning because he is at one with himself, or
as he himself is recorded as saying, 'The Father and I are one.' The
intimate group destroys Judas but even when it does its worst it cannot
undermine the trust of Jesus in his own identity.

Families and intimate groups nourish and sustain their members but
they can also inflict the most exquisite pain usually through the

---

[1]Christopher Bryant (1978) *The River Within*. London: Darton, Longman & Todd, p. 17.

withholding of love or through the creation of conditions for acceptance and approval. As a therapist I am regularly confronted by those who have suffered in this way and as a result are unable to experience their own value or to find meaning in the world. The state of self-rejection is alienation from the core of one's own being or, to use the other interpretation, it is separation from God who resides within. For me, therefore, the person who is caught up in self-rejection is experiencing hell. When Judas leaves the Upper Room he is in hell and he remains there until the end of his earthly life. It is a grim thought that he may have been driven there by a lack of love and understanding on the part of the other disciples and that the love of Jesus for him was ultimately powerless in the face of the indifference or even hostility of the others. I am reminded of clients who are clearly loved by perhaps mother or father but who can no longer perceive or experience that love and know only the jealousy, contempt or hate of their siblings.

When Jesus appears before the High Priest he is face-to-face with those who will use all the weight of their authority and the religious tradition that they represent in order to destroy him. They succeed in their intention insofar as they bring about his crucifixion but at another level they fail completely. They are totally unable to induce in Jesus those feelings of overpowering guilt that destroy the personality and leave an individual without hope of forgiveness. The purveyors of such annihilating guilt are often to be found in the ranks of the religious and again, as a therapist, I am all too familiar with their victims. Their viciousness resides in their ability to create a total view of reality (religions are customarily expected to explain everything) so that those in whom guilt has been induced have no way out of their predicament except abject capitulation. The therapist working with such a client has the painful and painstaking task of enabling the guilt-sufferer to dismantle, brick by brick, the edifice of the religious prison in which he or she is incarcerated. The work is rendered the more complex by the need to separate out the annihilating and inappropriate guilt induced by the religion-mongers from the healthy and appropriate guilt which unerringly points to those obstacles that are preventing individuals from making contact with the core of their own being. The God of this kind of religion, it seems, seldom bears much resemblance to the God whose presence is to be found within.

Jesus, in his confrontation with Pilate, encounters the embodiment of corrupt secular power and refuses to be intimidated. In the same way that he rejects the guilt-inducing power of the religious authorities, so, too, he refuses to enter into dialogue with Pilate. In some ways this demands even greater self-assurance for Pilate certainly believed that he had authority to release Jesus and, given reassuring noises, would undoubtedly have tried to do so. Colluding with those in power is a sure way of losing personal integrity and yet the process is often subtle and seductive. The lust for power lurks in the hearts and minds of even the most unlikely people and again the therapist meets with monotonous regularity those who have betrayed themselves for a whiff of power and prestige and no longer know how to retain their own identity. Such a fate often befalls those who are particularly gifted and have great talents to exercise for the good of the community. The sad tales of their often spectacular downfalls do much to help fill the columns of the gutter press. When Pilate is told that his power is worthless and that he has no real authority he hears what many discover through the personal tragedy of gaining an ephemeral power at the cost of their own souls.

The soldiers who carry out the act of crucifixion are trapped in a role from which there is no escape. I have suggested that Jesus himself was able to see beyond the role and to make contact with the people behind the military uniform; we might even take comfort from imagining that after the horrific events on Calvary the soldiers found a way of discovering personal liberty. Their predicament, however, illuminates the insidious way in which the roles that we assume can obscure us from others and even ourselves. We can become so caught up in playing the part of our occupation or professional persona that we lose our anchorage and turn into a caricature of a person, divorced from our centre. The role takes on its own authority whether or not we are literally under the authority of others, and in its name we fall into the habit of performing actions and even thinking thoughts that are nothing less than a succession of self-betrayals. In the last month I have shared the desperation of a man, distinguished and respected in his profession, who has made the shattering discovery that he is on the very edge of ultimate self-betrayal. He knows that he must resign his position and perhaps even leave his marriage for there, too, he realises that he is no more than an actor, a shell of a person who no longer knows where to locate the source of his being.

As we have followed Jesus through the stages of his Passion we have encountered a man able to withstand the rejection of his intimates, to refute the accusations of the religious authorities without succumbing to guilt, to turn his back on the seductive invitation to collude with corrupt power and to avoid the trap of confusing either himself or others with the roles that are enacted. In short, we discover a person who avoids with triumphant assurance the pitfalls into which so many clients coming for therapy have plunged headlong. Here is a man, in Christopher Bryant's words, who is clearly 'at one with his true centre and living in accordance with the truth of his own being'. It remains now to throw more light on why this is so and clearly it is not good enough simply to affirm that Jesus is the Son of God and would therefore by definition not require psychotherapy! If, as I have argued, we are all sons and daughters of God, it may not be without value to attempt a more penetrating study of our brother, Jesus, so that we may more readily perceive the way to human fulfilment and hence to the divinisation of the human family.

Chapter 8
The Personality of Jesus and the Process of Therapy

It is clear from the Gospel narratives that Jesus was a special person from the very moment of conception. Whatever we may or may not believe about angels, virgin births or the operation of the Holy Spirit, there can be no doubt that Mary and Joseph knew that their child was special. The place and manner of his birth may have been humble in the extreme but his welcome into the world was exceptional. The stories of adoring shepherds, rejoicing angels and worshipping Magi simply serve to reinforce the sense of wonder and celebration at the arrival of a precious and uniquely special human being into the world.

This, then, is what human beings deserve as they make their way into life but in our Western culture only a tiny number are lucky enough to experience even a pale reflection of such a welcome. The fortunate few have a mother who rejoices at their presence in her womb and is filled with a sense of joyful wonder at their coming into being. They have a father who surrounds the mother with loving protection and is prepared to take bold decisions when he senses that danger lurks for the unborn child. They are received into a wider community where their birth is a signal for celebration and delight. More commonly, however, the passage into life for the newborn is very different. Mothers are often anxious about or even hostile towards what is growing in their bodies. Fathers frequently have scant understanding of a woman's experience and afford little support or protection during the mother's months of pregnancy. In many cases today the wider community has no interest in the birth and even family bonds are often so tenuous in a highly mobile society that there can be no assurance of family involvement and support. The welcome into the world, in short, can be uncertain and in many instances there is only coldness or indifference. For some children their experience, far from being akin to that of Jesus, is more reminiscent of that of the Holy Innocents. Metaphorically they are murdered before they are two years old.

The sense of Jesus' specialness is still very much in evidence as he approaches adolescence. The story of the visit to the Temple in Jerusalem shows us a boy who is confident enough in himself to keep company with the scholars of the day and not be overawed by their authority. What is more, Mary and Joseph are able to overcome their own pain and anxiety at their son's apparent precociousness and lack of concern for their feelings; his mother is able to ponder these things in her heart and to be at peace with herself. This incident provides a remarkable insight into the family home in which Jesus grew up. Clearly he is not only deeply loved but also respected so that he is able to exercise the freedom to display his own remarkable gifts without fear of being adversely judged or rejected. One outcome of this, it seems, is that he does not find it difficult in turn to respect his parents and to be subject to their authority in most aspects of his daily existence.

The willingness to conform is at first sight surprising in one who is to become the most radical non-conformist in human history. Yet there seems little doubt that Jesus, for the most part, grew up in conformity with the conventions and practices of his day. He learned a trade (lovingly instructed perhaps by Joseph), worked as an ordinary member of society, attended the synagogue and was steeped in the tradition of his culture. It would seem, however, that this apparently conventional existence was serving all the while to nourish his inner sense of identity and to strengthen the deep sense of his unique vocation.

The concept of vocation often receives a poor press these days and yet it is evident that, from a very early age, Jesus was a person with a vision of his own meaning and purpose. This is not to suggest that he knew what it was he had to do in any precise terms and yet it is clear that his 'Father's business' was what informed his deepest longings. I am tempted to believe that persons who have been truly welcomed into the world and whose specialness is beyond any doubt in the eyes of those who love them have every chance of discovering a meaning and purpose. They become literally 'visionaries' in the sense of being drawn slowly and irresistibly towards the illumination of their own destiny.

It could be argued that, at the age of 30, Jesus was ready to fulfil the meaning of his life because up to that point he had experienced a totally exceptional validation of his being in the world. Treasured and respected by his parents from the moment of conception, he won a favoured place in his community through the development of his practical, social and intellectual skills. Certainly, by the time we hear of him at the marriage feast in Cana it is clear that he is socially assured and utterly at ease with his own authority. It seems, too, that he has a sense of fun as well as a natural sympathy for the predicament of others. The person who is about to embark on the life of the radical and charismatic outsider is literally the life and soul of the party.

It is also evident that Jesus was a highly articulate man. Not only is he steeped in the Jewish scriptures but he is capable of employing language to tell stories that draw their raw material from the world around him while infusing it with symbolic meaning of the profoundest intensity. In this sense Jesus is a poetic orator, capable of using language at its most richly expressive. But it is not only with groups and crowds that he shows himself to be so verbally accomplished. It is also clear that he is at home with the language of intimacy, for otherwise it is difficult to understand how he could have won such devoted affection from his followers and especially from the women among them. When after the resurrection we witness his meeting in the garden with the sorrowing Mary Magdalen we are in the presence of a man who can convey the deepest love simply by uttering the name of the beloved. The fact, too, that on this occasion he restrains Mary from physical embrace suggests that she had come to know him as a person whose physical responsiveness was as sensitive and spontaneous as his use of language. Language itself is stretched to breaking point when we ponder the amazing significance of Jesus as the incarnate Lord.

Perhaps the most daunting idea for anyone attempting to live out a Christian life is the suggestion that we are called to 'imitate' Christ. In some ways this notion is preposterous for clearly the society and culture of Jesus' time were utterly different to our own and to 'imitate' him might be to court a bizarre and anachronistic way of being that would render us eccentric in the extreme and alienate most of our contemporaries. At a deeper level, however, we are invited in faith to explore the furthest limits of our human potential and to discover what it might mean, like Jesus, to become fully human. In this sense, our goal is to celebrate our own identity with as clear an affirmation of unique personhood as that uttered by Jesus in his authoritative 'I am'. Such a celebration is the outcome not of self-centredness and self-absorption but of self-love which comes from acknowledging that in our innermost being we are acceptable and desirable to the God who sustains us.

As I pondered on the personality of Jesus and on what imitation might mean, I was suddenly and startlingly aware that I have chosen a profession where I catch unmistakable glimpses of my Lord every day of my working life. Recently, for example, I was awestruck as I read the account of the relationship one of my trainees is currently forging with a woman who experienced sexual abuse from her father and her brother throughout most of her adolescence. My awe springs from the realisation of the healing that is being wrought in and through this relationship and almost as a matter of course in both the client and in the trainee therapist who is seeking to be with her in her pain.

Like this sexually abused woman, many clients who arrive at the therapist's door have certainly never been welcomed into life. On the contrary they have often been rejected, ignored or unwanted. Gradually, however, as they begin to experience and to trust the therapist's acceptance and the validation that springs from the therapist's understanding and cherishing of them, so they begin to feel at home in the created world. Resentment and bitterness can be fully experienced and then exorcised so that they can begin to take their place in a society that, previously, they had both hated and feared. Such a reconciliation is often the prelude to the first glimmerings of personal uniqueness and the possibility of new meaning. In brief, acceptance by another leads to a sense of belonging to the wider society, which in turn engenders a level of self-acceptance from which the experience of personal uniqueness can spring.

My sense of being in a privileged profession is even further heightened when I consider how, in therapy, tongues are unloosed and language takes on a new and often mysterious beauty. Not only, it seems, do I glimpse my Lord but I also hear his voice. It is my experience that at the beginning of therapy a client is commonly unambitious in the use of language. Even when great distress pushes him or her into verbal expression that seems unstoppable, there is usually a pedestrian and repetitive quality about the language employed. As therapy proceeds, however, and the client risks confronting feelings in the present moment, there is often a perceptible shift in the use of words. Images and metaphors begin to abound and the client is concerned to seek the *mot juste* and to discover the adjective that most nearly describes the subtle nuance of meaning he or she wishes to convey or the elusive feeling which suddenly and unpredictably rises up from memories long since buried in the unconscious. Indeed there is a whole discipline of counselling called 'focusing' that encourages clients to track down a 'felt sense' and to find appropriate language to describe their discovery. It is not, I believe, unduly fanciful to suggest that when therapy is proceeding well the client gradually begins to extend the boundaries of his or her use of language and to discover an articulacy that had previously lain dormant or unexploited. One client once remarked to me that he had had no idea that he could talk 'like a poet' until he entered therapy and others have been genuinely startled by the images and metaphors that cross their lips in the course of a counselling session. It is as if language ceases to be a smokescreen for concealing the inner world of the person; instead it is transparent in the sense that it becomes the means through which the person is revealed to the world in all his or her complexity. Language is the sacred medium for the expression of wholeness.

For many clients in therapy it is not only language but also the body that is released into new life. The physical responsiveness of Jesus to those about him is seldom mirrored in the life of the conventional Christian congregation but for many Christians the sacrament of the Eucharist does at least provide a reminder that their faith is as much about the body as the soul. At the moment of communion they touch their Lord and are united to him as if in a physical embrace. The joy of being physically enfolded is too deep for words but where it is absent the pain, too, can be inexpressible. Such an absence commonly characterises many of those who find themselves in therapy and as I reflect on this I wonder whose presence is at work in the transformation of the body that I am so often moved to witness during the therapeutic process. It is not uncommon for the person who is struggling with deep and longstanding distress to feel alienated from his or her body and to respond stiffly and awkwardly to the overtures of others. Tightly crossed arms, clenched jaws and crossed legs are not infrequently the outward signs of the frightened and distrustful person. He or she cannot comfortably be at home in the body and has often found it necessary to cut off from physical (and sexual) sensations altogether. It is as if the experience of being 'incarnate' is too painful to be endured. As therapy proceeds, however, such people begin cautiously to relax and to let go. Some even experience an exquisitely painful tingling in their limbs as they allow life to flow into them. For me there often comes the precious moment when I know that it is appropriate to touch a client for the first time because now he or she is 'embodied' and no longer afraid. At that moment we enter into a deeper communion for we are 'in touch' as incarnate beings and can no longer deny our capacity to confer blessing on each other.

I am aware of the enormity of what I am saying in these reflections on the process of therapy. I am making the claim that therapeutic relationships, when they go well, have the potential for enabling people to become more 'Christ-like', to reveal more clearly their divine attributes. That is to say such relationships make it possible for human beings to feel welcomed into the world, to sense their uniqueness and their purpose, to discover the sacredness and the wonder of language and to celebrate their physical natures. I do not wish to retract these reflections because I believe them to be true. At the same time, however, I am acutely aware that therapy seldom leads people into calm waters or emotional serenity. Instead it seems frequently to bring about a suffering of a wholly different order to the pain and distress that may well have brought the client to therapy in the first place.

This new order of suffering is undoubtedly brought about through the operation of empathy. To be understood with love is the prelude to understanding with love. Empathy brings with it an expansion of consciousness that makes it increasingly impossible to be blind to the pain of others and to the anguish of the world. Not that others (or the world for that matter) necessarily welcome such an extension of consciousness. To be understood can be intolerable for it may bring with it the confrontation with annihilating guilt or the recognition of an inner life invaded and dominated by the forces of darkness. In the course of therapy, therefore, as a client is enabled to take the risk of extending loving understanding to himself and to others, so he learns what it means both to bear the pain of another's suffering and to experience utter rejection at the hands of those who in Blake's words cannot 'bear the beams of love'.

It is as I reflect on the Passion of Jesus, however, that the well-nigh inevitability of such a process becomes clear. Jesus, as we have seen, was as secure in his identity as any human being has ever been. He was welcomed into the world, loved devotedly, respected by his elders and fully integrated into the society and culture of his day. It was precisely this wholeness of being, however, that led him inexorably into suffering and death for it made him, in the words of the German poet, Rainer Maria Rilke, no longer at home in the interpreted world. As he came more and more to live out his vision and to follow the vocation demanded by his Father's business, so the world in which he found himself was increasingly unable to support his presence. The full humanness of Jesus in all its glory was finally an intolerable affront to those weighed down with guilt, anxiety, ambition, fear and the lust for power. What is more, the humanity of Jesus, which in its completeness revealed his divinity, was at the same time the manifestation of utter vulnerability. The life of Jesus Christ, the incarnate God, reveals that to be fully human means to embody a vulnerability that may well court and invite a wounding unto death.

Jesus was both a great lover and greatly loved. It is my experience that those who have found healing through a relationship with a therapist always discover that they, too, are loveable and capable of loving. They are able, often for the first time, to glimpse what it might mean to be fully human but with this discovery comes the vulnerability that inevitably accompanies the one who dares to love and be loved. It is for this reason that I now warn clients that they are embarking on a dangerous enterprise. Should it bring about not merely an alleviation of problems but a healing of their fragmented humanity then they, too, will no longer be at home in the interpreted world and will suffer the agony of their yearning for another home. To those who are bold or foolish enough to contemplate training as therapists I can only whisper words of love and caution, for their task is too awesome to bear overmuch scrutiny. It may seem a far cry from the counsellor's consulting room to the cross of dereliction. I am persuaded, however, that the distance between these may suddenly and unexpectedly narrow. Every time I sit down with my client I know that we risk glimpsing God in each other and that, if this should occur, we may be swept along our own Via Dolorosa. It is not always easy at such times to remember that Jesus made the 'one full, perfect and sufficient sacrifice, oblation and satisfaction for the sins of the whole world' and that we are called to be Easter people. Hope lies beyond despair and 'all shall be well'. In the familiar words of Mother Julian of Norwich we hear the confident assertion of one who prayed that she might be privileged to share in the suffering and death of her Lord and whose prayer was granted. It is her testimony that upholds me as I dare to enter into the mind of Jesus and it is her faith that sustains me as each day I utter those seemingly simple words, 'How can I be of help to you?'

PART II
Person-centred Counselling and the Spiritual Dimension

Introduction

The contents of Part II are made up, for the most part, of lectures and chapters that were specifically invited or commissioned by editors or bodies concerned to elicit from me a spiritual perspective on a therapeutic theme. Such invitations afforded me a welcome platform for exploring and elaborating my own professional and spiritual preoccupations and I remain grateful particularly to the long-suffering audiences who first afforded me their generous attention.

There are two exceptions. Chapter 11 is an extract from a lecture that was first delivered in 1983 and that I gave at my own instigation. It shows how more than 14 years ago I was discovering in the work of both Jung and Rogers a source of inspiration not only for my therapeutic work but also for my life as a Christian. It has been a surprise for me in recent years to receive numerous enquiries about the genesis of the text and of its whereabouts in the published literature. The fact is that it was never submitted for publication and has remained buried in my own achieves apart from a brief appearance some years ago in a French translation at a Paris conference. Belatedly, then, I include it here in the hope that it still retains a certain interest especially for the increasing number of person-centred therapists who seem drawn to the work of Jung and his approach to dreams and the unconscious.

The other exception is the extract from my book on Carl Rogers (Thorne, 1992), which constitutes Chapter 12. In the international community of person-centred scholars I am now being identified with those who see in the later work of Rogers the seeds for the future development of the approach. It is indeed my belief that had Rogers lived longer we would have seen a more elaborate articulation of his views on the mystical and transcendental nature of relationship and on the implications for person-centred therapy of this dimension. In this extract from my study of Rogers I attempt to predict how his work will be perceived 50 years from now. My conclusion has not pleased some of my colleagues.

Reference

Thorne B (1992) *Carl Rogers*. London: Sage.

Chapter 9
Counselling and the
Spiritual Journey[1]

It is common for older people to wonder – often ironically – what happened 'before all these counsellors were around'. The subtext to such comments is that, in previous generations, people showed more grit and determination and got on with their lives without whinging and without indulging in continual self-analysis. Perhaps there is some truth in this assertion but it leaves out of account, I believe, a number of important factors. Not least is the undeniable change in the social fabric of our communal life in the second half of the twentieth century. The 'mobile society' has in many areas destroyed the geographical reality of the extended family and the changes in social mores have more recently threatened the shaky stability of the so-called nuclear family, which in itself is but poor protection against the vicissitudes of the economy and political fashions. But if the fabric of society has undergone profound changes so, too, have many of the prevalent attitudes that underpinned the old order. In no sphere is this more dramatic than in attitudes to religion and, more recently, to medicine. The reasons behind these shifts in attitude are complex. They involve belief systems, changing responses to authority of all kinds and a growing scepticism about the efficacy and even the integrity of much conventional wisdom. The net result, however, is that for growing numbers in our society neither the priest nor the doctor any longer constitute trustworthy sources of knowledge or support. It is perhaps significant that, as far as ministers of religion are concerned, those who do still command allegiance, usually of an extreme kind, are wedded to a highly dogmatic brand of belief that brooks no argument and can lead to punitive exclusion if the 'believer' deviates from the 'truth' or gives expression to doubt. Only absolute authority, it seems, remains appealing (for some) in a world of almost infinite relativity.

---

[1]This lecture was given in Birkenhead Town Hall on 19 April 1997, on behalf of the Charity 'Time and Space' of which I am patron. Part of it, in slightly amended form, was subsequently incorporated into "Spiritual Responsibility in a Secular Profession" in I. Horton and V. Varma (eds) (1997) *The Needs of Counsellors and Psychotherapists* pp200–250 and is reprinted by permission of the publishers, Sage Publications Ltd.

Past responses to emotional and psychological distress

It may be that previous generations were emotionally and psychologically more resilient than we are today. We shall never know, although
there is plenty of evidence of the mental and physical suffering that
ruined many lives in the past. The stories that are recounted by many
older clients also explode the myth that emotional resilience was once
universal and that we are now witnessing the emergence of a degenerate
species that has lost its backbone. More relevant I suspect, are the shifts
in social structures and the changes in attitude to which reference has
been made above. It is my fantasy that in the past the confidential
sharing of pain and confusion (which is one way of defining the therapeutic activity) was more likely to take place within the family circle or in
the vicar's study or in the family doctor's surgery than it does today. It is
also, I believe, a tenable hypothesis that a sense of continuity and of
common reference points was a part of most people's framework of
reality until well into the twentieth century despite the advances of
science and technology and the devastation of war. This aided the
maintenance of individual identity and kept at bay some of the more
poignant existential questions that characterise the distress of many of
those who currently seek the help of therapists. Today there is for most
of us a sense of the inadequacy of many of the understandings and basic
assumptions that were until comparatively recently operative in society.
In his recent book *The Gutenberg Elegies* the American critic, Sven
Birkerts, puts it starkly and concisely: 'The maps no longer describe the
terrain we inhabit. There is no clear path to the future. We trust that the
species will blunder on, but we don't know where to. We feel imprisoned in a momentum that is not of our own making' (Birkerts, 1994).

The therapist as family, doctor and priest

Counselling and psychotherapy have been described as the impossible
profession and the description is apt enough if counsellors and therapists believe that they must satisfy the needs and yearnings of all their
clients. The work is even more daunting when it is perceived within the
context of the rapidly shifting sands that Birkerts graphically portrays.
After all, therapists are themselves no more than struggling representatives of the species that 'blunders on' without direction and with an
increasing sense of foreboding. Indeed, the task is so evidently impossible that the temptation is to give up altogether or to redefine the therapeutic activity in strictly limited but perhaps more realistic terms. The
cognitive behavioural therapists have learned this lesson well. They are
satisfied, for example, if they can enable a client to cope more effectively
with a phobia or develop a more assertive stance towards an oppressive

parent or employer. The establishing of well-defined and often short-term goals has become commonplace at the outset of many therapeutic 'contracts' and there is no doubt that this 'humble' approach often achieves results of a sort, preserves the therapist from *folie de grandeur* and presumably reduces somewhat the possibility of an embittered band of disillusioned clients. Settling for limited objectives would certainly seem a sensible policy and the therapist who wishes to sleep soundly at night might be well advised to pursue this path. It fits well, too, with the current obsession to prove the efficacy of therapeutic interventions through the production of tangible and irrefutable results. Funding bodies and their affiliated researchers long to believe in the existence of a world where it is known that such and such a therapy will 'cure' panic attacks in four sessions or chronic depression in six. The truth of the matter, however, is that such neat solutions are rare and that even when they seem to apply there is no guarantee that the client has found anything more than a temporary alleviation of pain or a provisional move from what Freud described long ago as 'neurotic misery' to 'common unhappiness'.

I am unwilling to opt for the limited role however 'sensible' and appealing. I confess to a desire to engage at a deeper and more influential level with my clients, while knowing that such a desire may be the result of an inflated assessment of my own importance and capacity or an indication of an unconscious masochism that may end in exhaustion and burnout. The implications of such possible folly are far reaching. The starting point is a willingness to acknowledge the nature of the challenges that clients have been presenting to me for almost 30 years. Of course, there are those who need little more than a friendly companion to stay around for a while so that decisions can be made or complicated situations untangled. It is a privilege to be invited into such persons' lives for a space and to share in their deliberations and dilemmas. They seem to be saying to me: 'Be a committed attentive listener so that I may discover what I truly feel and think and need to do.' If my professional life were spent entirely with people of this kind, I have little doubt that I should feel useful and perhaps content, even if in danger of courting complacency or occasional boredom.

The legacy of the last 30 years, however, is very much more complex. Many clients who have entered my life have stayed a long time (some are there still) and I am changed as a result of them. There are times when they have driven me to the brink of despair or compelled me almost in spite of myself to examine honestly the belief system to which I subscribe. Their voices reverberate in my mind and even if they have never uttered the precise words I ascribe to them, I know I am not mistaken in my interpretation of their demands. Some say: 'Love me.' Others cry out: 'Heal me.' Others again plead: 'Give me meaning.' There are those who have demanded all three at different times.

The therapist as lover, healer and provider of meaning suggests the impossible profession to beat all impossible professions and yet my experience tells me that this is what has been asked of me by many people for many years. What is more, such people are on the increase and it is ironic that their proliferation coincides with a time when the 'value for money' approach to health care means that, in the public sector, therapy, when it is available at all, is often restricted to short-term contracts with limited goals. It is unlikely that, in such an ethos, a client will be prompted to contract for love, healing and meaning to be delivered in six sessions. The therapist who accepted such a contract would in any case be guilty of the most irresponsible collusion with insane expectations.

My perception is perhaps simplistic but I am suggesting that as the family disintegrates, institutional religion declines and the medical profession loses some of its credibility and much of its authority, those who seek love, healing and meaning do not know where to turn. The counsellor and psychotherapist offer hope: here are the potential substitute family members, doctors and priests for an age where, to quote Birkerts again, 'our post-modern culture is a vast fabric of competing isms: we are leaderless and subject to the terrors, masked as the freedoms, of an absolute relativism' (Birkerts, 1994). If we therapists accept that this is indeed the case and that a new and apparently impossible role has been thrust upon us, we are faced with an agonising dilemma. Do we run away altogether from such a daunting prospect, do we reject the role and adopt another as our economic masters seem to require or do we refuse to submit to panic and look the unpalatable truth in the face? Interestingly enough, in a telling paragraph in his prophetic analysis of our plight, Sven Birkerts incites us to face what may be our new vocation. 'Where the Virgin was once the locus of spirit and care,' he writes, 'the protectress of the interior life, the new site of power, now secular, is the office of the trained therapeutic specialist' (Birkerts, 1994).

The therapist as 'believer', in a disintegrating culture

I like the metaphor of the therapist as the protector of the interior life and as the locus of spirit and care. These are words with which I can identify. Such a person, it seems to me, does not cut an altogether foolish figure in the face of someone who yearns for love, or healing or meaning. Nor is he or she anything other than supremely important in a world that is increasingly cut off from beauty, simplicity, passion and the spiritual. Thus encouraged, I can look the unpalatable facts in the face and discover, as Carl Rogers once proposed, that perhaps they are friendly after all.

To brass tacks then. What does it mean to accept that as a therapist I shall be sought out by those who desire love, healing and meaning? How can I possibly equip myself for such encounters? These are the questions to which the rest of this lecture addresses itself in various ways. For the moment I offer some initial but fundamental reflections.

In the first place, I must rid myself of the grandiose idea that I can give love, healing or meaning to anyone, let alone that it is my professional duty to do so. Any gift, however precious, is ultimately useless unless it is treasured and received by the one to whom it is offered. I am dependent on the other to receive and this in turn will be determined by the quality of our relationship. Secondly, I must renounce any pretension I might entertain to be the sole or even principal provider or source of love, healing or meaning for another individual. However deep the yearning may be, if I set myself up as the ultimate response to it, I am likely to be the cause of disillusionment or, at worst, of abuse. What, then, can I do? I would suggest that I can attend with the utmost seriousness to my own belovedness, to my own healing and to the meaning of my own life. If I do this I shall not be afraid in the presence of the other's yearnings and demands nor shall I be tempted to use the other's needs as a means of filling my own emptiness. Attending to my own belovedness will entail an openness in my personal relationships that allows others to nourish me. It will also require of me a willingness to be cherished by the natural environment and by the spiritual forces that surround me. Attending to my own healing will entail a refusal to be anything other than my whole self, to insist on acknowledging my essential unity as body, mind and spirit and not to submit to fragmentation. Attending to the meaning of my own life will require a preparedness to stay closely in touch with the day-to-day pressures of my own living and to relate these to what I profess to believe about human beings and the nature of reality. It will also require a continual monitoring of my beliefs about the therapy I practise and a commitment to living them out in my work rather than simply mouthing them at professional conferences and seminars. If all this sounds like a stern discipline it should come as no surprise. How otherwise could it be possible to welcome into a relationship those who yearn for love, healing or meaning without the fear of being eaten alive or of succumbing to an annihilating despair? As our materialistic and increasingly electronic culture embraces a network of communications where the interior life is sacrificed on the altar of efficiency and to the shallowness of the instant response, so the counsellors and psychotherapists must commit themselves to a deeper level of experiencing. For my own part I have concluded that, without such commitment, the only honest thing to do would be to trade in my professional diplomas and seek alternative employment.

The need for meaning: spirituality, religion and psychology

One of the more intriguing developments among therapists in recent years has been the change of attitude towards notions of spirituality and the spiritual dimension of personality. Therapists who a decade or so ago would have scoffed at such preoccupations have now acknowledged their relevance and in many cases have been forced to review their own understanding of human nature and human destiny. This change is undoubtedly partly attributable to the manifest existential needs of clients referred to above and to the increasing willingness on the part of some to articulate their need for meaning and to insist on therapists engaging with them in this exploration. Although there are still therapists who tend to perceive spiritual concerns –especially if they touch on matters concerning life after death or unspecified spiritual forces – as evidence of neurosis or even incipient psychosis, such practitioners, it would seem, are either on the decrease or have become much less vocal in their views. It would be wrong, however, to see this shift in attitude as being entirely client-driven. There is I believe something of a sea-change taking place within the fields of both psychology and theology that is resulting in a developing dialogue that would have been unthinkable until very recently. It is significant for example that a lectureship has been endowed (by a successful novelist specialising in spiritual matters) in the Faculty of Divinity of Cambridge University for the study of science and religion and that the first incumbent is a clinical psychologist who also happens to be an Anglican priest! In 1994, too, the respected journal *American Psychologist* carried a major article on psychology and religion. Its author, Dr Stanton Jones, had this to say:

'It seems that psychology is, in American society, filling the void created by the waning influence of religion in answering questions of ultimacy and providing moral guidance' (Jones, 1994). Later in the same article he quotes an earlier writer, Browning, who observed: 'Traditional religion and modern (therapeutic) psychology stand in a special relation to one another because both of them provide concepts and technologies for the ordering of the interior life' (Browning, 1987).

The needs of clients, the signs of a tentative dialogue between religion and psychology and the ravages of competitive materialism all contribute to the creation of a climate where it is becoming increasingly difficult for the therapist to avoid adopting a stance towards spiritual experience. There would seem to be at least three possible positions to take up. He or she can deny the reality of spirituality and see so-called spiritual phenomena as ultimately explicable in psychological terms and therefore not requiring an alternative framework for their conceptualisation. A second position is to acknowledge the validity of spiritual experi-ence but to exclude it from the therapeutic arena on the score that counsellors and psychotherapists are not equipped to respond to it and have more pragmatic behavioural, cognitive and affective objectives to achieve. The third position is to accept spiritual experience as one of the 'givens' of being human and to engage fully with it. What is not possible any longer is for a therapist of integrity to duck the question altogether. The rest of this lecture may be heard as the reflections of a therapist who long ago realised that he could not be a spiritual being in church and someone else in the consulting room. The 'I' who is/am a secular counsellor is/am a spiritual being and if that is true of me it is by definition true of each and every client who comes to meet me.

Mystics, 'magic moments' and the Garden of Eden

There is a well-known story of a devout French peasant who spent several hours each day before the altar of the village church. What puzzled people was that he seemed to do nothing during these lengthy periods; he did not ply his rosary, he was not apparently praying, he read no devotional books. He simply sat there gazing into space – or so it appeared. Finally curiosity got the better of his fellow-villagers and one of them asked him bluntly: 'Pierre, what do you do every day in the church?' The old man smiled and said, 'Well, I looks at 'im and 'e looks at me.'

I have never before tried to define a mystic but I suspect that old Pierre was a mystic right enough for as I understand it all mystics are lovers and are singularly untrammelled by the confines of time. They have the capacity to move into a realm of being where the invisible is as real as the visible, if not more so, and where the yearning for relationship with the 'divine' is given priority. The mystic, in short, inhabits the vast terrain of the worlds of the visible and the invisible, the past, present and future, and lives there permeated by a longing and a yearning for a relationship with the source of all love.

The trouble, of course, is that we have come to think of the mystics as a race apart, a special breed who can have little of importance to convey to us ordinary mortals. My contention is that this is a most unfortunate notion that elevates the mystic in a most inappropriate fashion and demeans the rest of humanity quite unjustly. That is why I like peasant Pierre. He is clearly not a high flyer; he is not an intellectual giant or a spiritual virtuoso. He is a peasant who likes going into church to pursue a relationship with God by gazing at a closed Tabernacle that conceals the sacrament of Christ's body, which in turn conceals the personhood of God. And in the hiddenness he sees. What is concealed is revealed to his eyes and he is enraptured.

From time to time, of course, many of us get whiffs of a world behind or beyond the one we normally accept as the context of our existence. We are struck by extraordinary coincidences, we have sudden premonitions, we are convinced of presences, we are overwhelmed by sudden feelings of love or oneness. Or, if we are not so lucky, we are caught up in fearful anxieties, we sense the appalling power of evil, we are plunged into the most unimaginable despair. At the time such experiences feel very real and they may affect us profoundly but somehow we fail to integrate them into our concept of reality. They remain as 'coincidences' or 'feelings that came over me' or 'peculiar sensations'. We are unlikely to say to ourselves, let alone to others, that we have entered a world infinitely more extensive and astonishing than the workaday reality to which we are normally confined. To do so would be to run the risk of appearing crazy in the eyes of others or, perhaps more sinister, to begin to question our own sanity or stability.

I want to suggest that the time has come when we must stop being such cowards and allow the data of our own experiencing to be openly acknowledged and explored. If we have it within our power to become mystics then we need to take ourselves seriously and to see what the implication might be of developing such potential.

For me, my confrontation with my mystical self has frequently come about through my work as a therapist. Both in individual counselling and in group work I have often experienced what I call 'magic moments'. Such moments signify a particular intensity of relating in which a new level of understanding is achieved and a sense of validating freedom experienced by both client and counsellor. The surge of well-being that follows such moments is almost indescribable. Outwardly situations probably remain unaltered and the client's problems, for example, may be as insoluable as ever. And yet everything is different because love has been tapped into and a new reality has been experienced. Often such magic moments seem to have resulted from the acceptance of powerlessness, which is not a sign of resignation but of a positive stance that unites counsellor and client and leads to a waiting without hope but also without despair. I want to say a bit more about this because I find it exciting.

To start with I believe that the acceptance of powerlessness is a rare attitude in our culture. We tend to be an 'I'll fix it' lot who like to think that there is an answer to every problem (to be provided by an expert). We can actually become very frustrated and even angry when no solution seems to be forthcoming. True, we may be resigned to things, but this is not the state of mind I am attempting to describe, for resignation is usually tinged with a certain amount of bitterness or gentle despair. The acceptance of powerlessness of which I speak is recognition of our own limitations and at the same time acknowledgement of the infinite resources by which we are surrounded. Unfortunately, however, there is nothing we can do by straining or striving to lay hold of these resources. What is more, access to them seems almost impossible if we remain unaccompanied. Perhaps it is the mark of those whom we have come to recognise as the greatest mystics that they are apparently able to experience directly the companionship of God, although it is worth recalling that for many of them much of their lives was or is spent enduring his apparent absence. Be that as it may the fact is, I believe, that most of us do not apprehend God directly – we cannot bank upon this direct companionship with God. Instead we have to make do with each other but – and here is the crucial point – it is in acknowledging the infinite value of such companionship that we are enabled to accept our powerlessness and thus to make ourselves accessible to the infinite resources by which we are surrounded.

If all that sounds very fanciful or unintelligible let me illustrate what I mean by drawing on concrete examples. In a book published in 1987 called *Key Cases in Psychotherapy* I wrote at length about one particular relationship with a client called Sally. This relationship, which continued over a number of years, was characterised by a quite remarkable mutuality that resulted in a level of trust quite unlike that of any other therapeutic relationship which I had previously experienced. It meant, among other things, that Sally and I were able to acknowledge stuckness and powerlessness. I did not feel that I had to be the 'good' therapist providing all the right answers or facilitating all the right developments and Sally gave up all notion of playing the part of the 'good' client whose task it was to grow and self-actualise. When we were stuck and did not know what to do we simply accepted this and instead of getting frightened or frustrated we stayed close to each other and waited. The staying close was, of course, critically important and often it was symbolised by holding hands or by embracing each other. In short, our powerlessness was shared in a context of love and caring for each other. There was no element of judgement or expectation on either side. It was a waiting without hope and yet without despair. The outcome of such waiting was usually entirely creative and often quite unexpected. Sometimes, apparently without rational connection, one or other of us would find an image or a sentence coming to us and we would be bold enough to express it. Sometimes we found ourselves communicating to each other in physical ways that, to an outside observer, might have seemed comical or even outrageous. Sometimes tears would flow silently or Sally would experience an intense and intolerable pain. On occasions I would find myself leaping up and fetching a book from my shelves in order to discover a particularly powerful passage that had just returned to my memory. From the sharing of powerlessness in a context of love, our waiting became the prelude to the discovery of a treasure house of resources both within ourselves and without. I have no hesitation in describing such a waiting as a waiting upon God.

And then there was another woman whom I will call Teresa. She had suffered for years from cyclical depression that had sometimes kept her housebound for weeks. In our relationship, however, the depression

had been largely absent and much of the time there had been the excitement for Teresa of discovering new energy and relationships, a great
delight in life and a sense of emerging purpose. Then one day she
arrived apparently in terror and displayed all the symptoms of an incipient psychotic breakdown. Her eyes stared, she thrust her knuckles into
her mouth in anxiety, she moved physically like a startled hare. Her
words were incoherent and her appearance was dishevelled. I did not
know what to do and I was utterly taken aback by this sudden turn of
events. For a time I accused myself of lacking perception and wondering
how on earth I could have imagined that this client was making
progress. There was a moment when I was within an ace of telephoning
the Health Centre and requesting them to summon an ambulance. And
yet behind it all and in the depth of my own being I sensed a deep peace,
a kind of cosmic 'all rightness'. I found myself gradually moving deeper
into this 'all right' place and finding there, as with Sally, that I loved
Teresa and being pretty certain that she loved me. It would be all right to
wait. After half an hour she got up and left, rather abruptly, and disap-
peared from the building. Something told me, however, that she had not
gone far and sure enough I found her sitting on the ground against the
wall of the Counselling Service building with her head in her hands. She
looked up as if expecting me and we held hands very tightly. She half
smiled and told me she would be all right. I believed her and left her
almost at once to return to my next client. The next day Teresa appeared
looking more vibrant than I had ever seen her and fully restored to her
emerging self. Again it seemed that the stature of this kind of waiting had
revealed itself in all its immensity.

I want to claim, I suppose, that the kind of experiences I have just
described with Sally and Teresa are, in fact, mystical experiences. They
are characterised by a context of mutual love, an acceptance of powerlessness and a refusal to be coerced into premature action, an utter
absence of judgement and expectation and a deep if largely unexpressed
belief that there are more resources in heaven and earth and in ourselves
than we could ever conceive. What I have not so far mentioned is the
accompanying sense of being quite outside of time. For me there is an
entry into a new region of experiencing where there is an absence of
anxiety and guilt. I do not think that I had previously connected this
absence with the sense of timelessness but as I ponder on the matter the
relationship becomes increasingly obvious. It only takes a moment's
thought to realise that we are usually anxious about something we have
done or about something we fear is going to happen. Anxiety attaches
itself either to the past or the future. Guilt similarly springs from actions
performed in the past resulting in a present state of being that fears
adverse judgement in the future. Anxiety and guilt, in short, make it
impossible for us to be anything other than fearful creatures dreading
the future and regretting the past. In such a state we are scarcely likely to

be able to take our place in the eternal now. When we succeed in doing that then we shall have heeded the biblical injunction to 'be not anxious for the morrow for the morrow will look after the things of itself.'

It is not, I am sure, unimportant that many of my most powerful experiences as a therapist have come about with women. It seems to me that in our culture, at least, the potential for guilt and anxiety is greatly intensified when a man and a woman are alone together. To banish guilt and anxiety from such relationships is to create an altogether new arena and it is perhaps not surprising that in such a context healing forces of undreamed of magnitude can be released. Sexuality has, of course, been a prime cause for untold guilt and anxiety in our culture. Christian theology – and particularly the Church Fathers (rightly and sinisterly so named) – have much to answer for. Many women seem to be born feeling guilty and when they experience themselves as sexual beings the feelings of guilt intensify and proliferate. At the present time the apparent escalation in sexual offences and particularly in cases of rape and violent abuse has added intense feelings of anxiety and fear to the cauldron of guilt. In day-to-day terms this often means that a woman finding herself alone with a man is thrown into a turmoil of powerful emotions. She may experience feelings of desire and attribute them to a perverted nature that is intent on the seduction and manipulation of men. Or she may feel afraid and terrifyingly vulnerable and is then likely to perceive men as beasts of prey against whom she must defend herself, perhaps to the extent of withdrawing from male company altogether. In short, she is likely to be a bundle of guilt and anxiety and men, in their turn, are often unlikely by their own behaviour to do much to improve this situation. On the contrary, many men are apparently only too happy to be seduced while others are quite prepared to use women for their own sexual release. The man who exhibits deep empathy and tender-ness is a rare being, it seems, and even he is not infrequently suspected of an ulterior motive.

The woman's experience of being corrupt runs deep and afflicts those who certainly have no conscious religious affiliations. The daugh-ters of Eve seem to have paid dearly for the supposed sin of their arche-typal mother and perhaps the most dreadful outcome is that they often distrust their own loving. Even as mothers many women now feel themselves to be abject failures and much modern psychological insight encourages them to take the blame for the aberrant development of their offspring. It is my contention that in the context of a relationship where a woman can feel her love to be accepted and acceptable without experiencing herself as a manipulator and without having sexual and emotional demands made upon her in return, then she is freed from the stigma of corruption and becomes the most potent healing force both for herself and for others. That, I believe, is what happened with Sally and Teresa. Both felt love for me and knew that I treasured and accepted that love without feeling manipulated by it. What is more they knew that I demanded nothing in return. As a result they became a source for my healing as well as for their own.

In the Garden of Eden, you recall, there was no guilt or anxiety. Adam and Eve were perfect companions and they had no shame. They wandered naked but, remember, the Lord God also walked in the Garden in the cool of the evening. All the resources were available to them. What if that was actually still the case? Supposing the Fall – and I have come to think of this recently in terms not of our being banished from the Garden but of God being rejected as too awesome, too holy – has been remedied (and that, incidentally is the claim of Christianity). Supposing – just suppose – that we are creatures of eternity and that if we can be true companions to each other, then all the resources necessary for our healing and our well-being are accessible to us. I am coming increasingly to believe that such is indeed the case. From time to time, as I experience my 'magic moments', I would go so far as to say that I know that it is the case. I do not mean that we shall not know physical death but for timeless creatures death can be of no significance. Nor does death constitute the antithesis of healing. Healing of whole persons may indeed sometimes take the form of sickness or death as part of its process. To return to old Pierre with whom we began, it is clear that death held no fears for him. In some ways it might even be imagined that he yearned for it. And yet, for those who already see face-to-face and for whom the resources for healing are already accessible, death is neither to be feared nor to be desired. It is but part of life whose essence is timeless. Heaven is about us always. It is we who insist on banishing ourselves from the Garden.

References

Birkerts S (1994) The Gütenberg Elegies. Boston: Faber & Faber.
Browning D (1987) Religious Thought and Modern Psychologies. Fortress: Philadelphia.
Jones SL (1994) A constructive relationship for religion with the science and profession of psychology. American Psychologist 49(3): 184–99.
Thorne B (1987) Beyond the core conditions. In Dryden W (ed) Key Cases in Psychotherapy. London: Croom Helm, pp 44–77.

Chapter 10
The Accountable Therapist: Standards, Experts and Poisoning the Well[1]

When I write, I usually have something to say about which I feel strongly and that I believe I can articulate with reasonable clarity and persuasiveness. Indeed, much of my pleasure comes from presenting a well-documented and lucid argument with passion. In this instance, however, I find myself in a rather different mood. Instead of clarity, I shall present my confusion and in order to do that I fear I shall have to inflict a certain amount of autobiographical data upon my reader. Indeed, I have a somewhat unnerving sense that I am embarking on a process of self-therapy in public. Perhaps, though, readers will not be too dismayed at being cast in the role of eavesdroppers, even of voyeurs – legitimate snoopers into the somewhat bewildered psyche of a battle-scarred person-centred counsellor.

Essentially I have felt for some years now like a man who is in danger because he has become imprisoned in the profession of therapy. Let me attempt to explain. This summer I shall have completed 29 years as a counsellor and that is a long haul judged by any criterion. During that time I have experienced astonishing developments in the world of therapy and counselling in our country and in a minor way I suppose I have contributed to some of them. When I began as a counsellor in 1968 there was no Association for Student Counselling, there was no British Association for Counselling, there was certainly no UK Council for Psychotherapy. The man whom I still regard as the greatest therapist I ever met – George Lyward of Finchden Manor – possessed no formal qualifications as a therapist and put MA(Cantab) after his name in the conviction – wholly justified it seemed – that this would be sufficient evidence for any discerning person that he was wholly competent at the

---

[1]The first draft of this paper was originally presented as a lecture at the Annual Meeting of the Ashby Trust in 1991 and subsequently published in *Self and Society* 23(4), September 1995. In its present form it constitutes Chapter 111–1 in House R, Totton N (eds) (1997) *Implausible Professions*. Ross-on-Wye: PCCS Books. It is reprinted with permission of the publishers.

job. Nobody seemed to worry much that his Cambridge degree was in history. There were, of course, some powerful analysts around who held mysterious court in Hampstead, and those were the days of the Tavistock ascendancy and of residential weeks in pursuit of leadership skills where Tavistock-trained consultants traumatised business men and academics alike by their sometimes impenetrable interpretations of group process and their disciplined regard for the second hand of their watches. But, on the whole, those few counsellors and therapists around had only rudimentary support systems, strange hybrid trainings and little sense of belonging to a greater body of brothers and sisters. What I remember vividly, however, was the sense of dedication and of adventure: the exhilaration of being pioneers in a new world. In 1989 I was invited to contribute to a book entitled *On Becoming a Psychotherapist* and was confronted by the somewhat daunting task of recalling my own training and the first months in my new and, at that time, almost unknown profession (Dryden and Spurling, 1989). In fact, the writing proved to be a thoroughly enlivening experience for it put me in touch again with the motivational energy, which constituted the driving force behind my aspirations of those days. In the first place, I did not recall being particularly excited as I set out for my training course. On the contrary, there was more a sense of being pulled somewhat against my will towards a kind of inevitable destiny. I knew that to become a counsellor meant giving up much that I loved dearly for I was a gifted teacher and could have looked forward to a pretty successful career, I think, in the teaching profession. Secondly, I recall clearly my determination not to be sucked into a kind of psychological ghetto; I was keen, for example, to retain my literary and theological interests and not to lose those perspectives on reality that had underpinned my life for so long. In short, I was highly resistant to any notion of a psychological framework for human personality and human interaction that would negate my understanding of persons as *essentially mysterious beings who shared in the overarching mystery of the cosmos.* I entered lectures on psychological theories of personality fortified by Wordsworth's Intimations of Immortality:

> Our birth is but a sleep and a forgetting:
> The soul that rises with us, our life's star, hath had
> elsewhere its setting and cometh from afar . . .
>   . . . trailing clouds
> of glory do we come from God who is our home.

Fortunately for me it turned out that my training did not constitute an assault on my previously held convictions and understandings. On the contrary it deepened them, added to them and gave them a new coherence and potency. The good fortune, as I see it, was that I was being trained to be a client-centred counsellor in the tradition of Carl Rogers.

As I read Rogers' books with increasing enthusiasm, I realised that I was not being asked to take on board a whole new perception of reality or a highly complex theory of human personality. I was not even being required to change my basic way of being with those who sought my help. Instead, I found in Rogers someone who seemed to esteem the validity of my own experience and who gave names to attitudes and behaviours that I had falteringly attempted to embody for many years. And so it was that Carl Rogers became for me, not the new guru or a source of all wisdom for the aspiring therapist, but a gentle companion who spoke of unconditional positive regard, empathy and genuineness, and this gave shape to what for me had previously been an almost instinctive and somewhat incoherent response to others in need.

The client-centred or person-centred approach not only enabled me to retain a firm hold on my own identity but went some way towards preserving me from arrogance and from the insidious snares of psychological power mongering. Weighty theories about personality development and complex maps of the unconscious certainly have their fascination but they can make those who have studied them feel important and erudite. Such a training would, I think, have been bad for me for I was only too aware that I was a powerful person and anything that might have added to that sense of power would probably have knocked my humility for six for a long time to come. In effect, I was being trained to reject the role of the expert and to become proficient at the far more delicate task of being the faithful companion. As I look back on that training experience and as I think now of my work as a trainer of person-centred therapists I have no doubt whatever that the whole enterprise is concerned with mutuality, with intimacy, with power sharing, with transparency, with tapping into currents of love and creativity that are the essence of spiritual reality. The expertise, if that is the appropriate word, lies in the capacity, to quote Scott Peck's words, 'to extend oneself for the purpose of nurturing one's own or another's spiritual growth' (Peck, 1978, p. 199).

Over the years I have come to acknowledge that all my most challenging clients have drawn me inexorably into the same terrain. They have, in fact, challenged my ability to love. It is notable that in the vast corpus of professional literature that now exists on counselling and psychotherapy there is not much reference to this issue of love. And yet I have known for many years that, for me, offering the core conditions of acceptance, empathy and congruence, if I do so consistently and honestly, means a willingness to love my clients and the likelihood that I shall end up doing so. I would go further: my experience has convinced me that it is, in fact, essential for me to love my clients if genuine healing is to occur and that the deeper the wound or the greater the deficiency the more likely it is that I shall have to extend myself in love to a degree that is costly in effort and commitment. There is part of me that does not like that conclusion. There are times when I would prefer my success as a therapist to depend on my knowledge, my therapeutic skills or techniques, my experience, my years of self-exploration. But I know that I should be deluding myself to believe that. Perhaps I have now run across too many incompetent therapists who are loaded with degrees and qualifications, or have undergone lengthy training analyses. However, love that finds its expression in 'the will to extend one's self for the purpose of nurturing one's own or another's spiritual growth' cannot permit fusion or the falling in love that leads to all kinds of sexual complications. The love to which I refer, in fact, is very demanding in the discipline it imposes. I must confess that I often find it difficult to see why a therapist without a belief in the potential divinisation of humanity and therefore in a divine source of power should submit himself or herself to such a discipline. It may be, however, that what I have described as the longing for the spiritual growth of another can be experienced as a profound and unselfish desire for a fellow human being to become fully human. For me this amounts to the same thing but I can readily appreciate that for many therapists the change in language is important. I am persuaded, too, but less readily, that a deep and unshakable yearning for the fulfilment of another's humanity need not be linked to a belief in God or indeed to any 'religious' interpretation or reality.

Having 'come clean' about this primacy of love in the therapeutic enterprise I do not wish to be accused of naïveté or sentimentalism. Love, as I mean it in this context, clearly demands the most rigorous training and discipline and levels of self-knowledge and self-acceptance that are unlikely to be attained without effort except by the most fortunate and beloved of persons. In short, I believe that counsellors need high-quality training, regular and sensitive supervision and every opportunity to extend and deepen their personal and professional resources. Events of recent years, however, lead me to write these words with a heavy heart and with a persistent sense of foreboding. Here lies the crux of the disquiet to which I referred at the beginning. Increasingly I have found myself becoming imprisoned in a vicious circle of feverish activity as the new accountability culture permeates the world of therapy. Now, it seems, we must not only do good work but manifestly be seen to do it and we must also seek to convince the public at large and the government in particular that we are worthy people, wholly reputable and dripping with prestigious qualifications that ensure our legitimacy and our continuing employability.

All this is very painful for me. As long ago as 1977 I was a prime mover in establishing a rigorous procedure for the accreditation of student counsellors. It was my conviction that we owed it both to our clients and to ourselves to aim for the highest possible standards and to challenge ourselves to become ever more open to personal and professional development. Little did I guess at that time that only 20 years later we should find ourselves caught up in an increasingly vicious circle where accountability, appraisal, evaluation, value for money, raising of standards, open competition and the like are the buzz words. Our culture has become virtually obsessed with seeing the world through the eyes of cost accountants and other measurers of human effectiveness where effectiveness often seems to mean the ability to persuade others to think and to do what, left to their own volition, they would never dream of thinking or doing – and to do it cheaply. I believe that we have witnessed a political transformation in the last two decades that has produced a society where more and more people are seeking the help of counsellors and therapists because of the stress caused by competitiveness, constant surveillance and the fear of failure. At the same time the therapists to whom they take their concerns are themselves increasingly fussed about their legitimacy, their performance, their cost effectiveness, the approval of government or, at a more mundane level, their acceptability to insurance companies. When someone told me a few years ago that the new Archbishop of Canterbury was also into appraisal and parish audits I experienced a wave of despair that threatened to engulf me altogether. Could it be that a priest will soon be evaluated on the quality of his sermons, the beauty of his singing, the numbers in the pews, the health of his marriage? Not so, it will be argued, for such appraisal will lead to a new level of self-exploration and a real sense of caring by senior clergy for their less experienced colleagues. It was shortly after the Archbishop's reported penchant for appraisal was made public that a Diocesan Bishop and his Suffragans informed the world that they had embarked upon just such an appraisal process and that its benefits and fruits were wondrous to contemplate. Men in the pews, too, were only too keen to point out that they, in the world of business and commerce, had long since been swept up into the appraisal, accountability culture and that it was about time the vicar had a dose of what it was like in the 'real' world.

As so often that splendid journal *The Tablet* came to my rescue. Talking about higher education it likened what was happening there to many other areas of our national life. The universities and polytechnics had allowed themselves to become infected, said *The Tablet*, with 'the language of the grocer's shop'. As a result, higher education was in danger of losing its soul (20 May, 1989). These phrases struck me as describing with disturbing accuracy much of what I experienced as a university counsellor. For many academics and administrators there has been an almost total transformation in the ethos of academic life and they find themselves caught up in a competitive ratrace where, not only can departments be swept into internecine strife, but individual worth is construed almost entirely in terms of research output or the ability to attract funds. Many staff who entered upon their careers with a genuine love of scholarship and the pursuit of knowledge find that there is no longer a place for them unless they are prepared to develop the skills and the mentality of the entrepreneur. Students, for their part, can, in such an environment, quickly cease to experience themselves as persons and become rather consumers of knowledge. And so it is that they come to the counsellor's office obsessed with the production of the perfect essay or paralysed with anxiety that they might not achieve the first class degree that, alone, can bolster their dehumanised self-concepts. The consumerist mentality and language of the grocer's shop has so infected the personality that soul has fled and left only a barren identity preoccupied with achievement and the concomitant fear of failure. Not infrequently, now, I find myself viewing counselling services in higher education as monasteries of a new dark age for they keep alive the vision of a world where persons matter more than things and where mutuality and understanding are more important than achievement and competition.

The danger is that the therapists themselves will collude by capitulating to the consumerist ideology and putting all their energy into ensuring that they are offering a good product, and by proving by their words and actions that they are intent on serving loyally in the brave new world of the managerial interest. And gradually and insidiously – perhaps without ever realising it – we, too, shall lose our own souls and become gloriously efficient at enabling our clients to function competently in a world devoid of meaning where all that matters is what we do, how we perform and the impressive range of our material possessions. Hence, my dilemma and my anxiety.

One of my later contributions at the end of the 1980s to the raising of standards was my co-chairmanship of the BAC Working Group on the Recognition of Counselling Courses. In many ways this was a wonderful experience as for three years with a group of much-loved and respected colleagues I struggled away at establishing criteria and processes for the evaluation of courses. It was stimulating, enjoyable and, what is more, I felt proud of our results. But now I am aware of the agony and the heartache that have been caused to many trainers up and down the land who, sometimes for reasons beyond their control, can never hope to have their courses recognised. Similarly I see the frequent adverts in the national press where applicants are required to have BAC accreditation, or to be eligible for it, before their candidature can even be considered. Where, I ask, is the soul in all this? Could it be that all the energy I have devoted over the years to schemes for accreditation and recognition, all the many hours spent in committee and in working parties, could it be that all this instead of improving the quality of therapy and enhancing the well-being of both therapists and clients has led, instead, to the creation of an exclusive professionalism and added anxiety, competitiveness and the fear of judgement to the lives of those who were previously lovingly and conscientiously responding to the needs of their clients? Have I, in fact, played right into the hands of those who have neurotically created this death-dealing culture of accountability and appraisal where the basic assumption is that nobody is really trustworthy and where everyone has to be monitored and given incentives if they are to do a good job? I am genuinely bewildered by these questions and there are times when they threaten to tear me in two. Sometimes I feel that my own therapeutic tradition makes things ten thousand times worse for me. I am committed to my client's path which he or she alone is capable of discovering given that I am equally committed to offering my unconditional acceptance, my empathy and my own transparent genuineness. As a therapist I am resolutely opposed to the imposition of external standards, to the passing of judgements, to the formulation of clever interpretations. By word and behaviour I attempt to convey my validation of the uniqueness of the individual and to counter the conditioning that for so many people has led to a sense of inferiority, inadequacy or even worthlessness. And yet in my professional arena my name has – with justification – become associated with accreditation, with the application of rigorous standards, with external judgements. Even as I write I am conscious that in a month's time I shall be attending the next meeting of the Executive Committee of the United Kingdom Register of Counsellors on which I faithfully serve.

Many years ago in an essay entitled 'Beyond the Core Conditions' I described my work with a particular client called Sally for a book entitled *Key Cases in Psychotherapy* (Dryden, 1987). The object of the book was to invite therapists of many different traditions to focus on therapeutic relationships that had proved maximally challenging and had revolutionised their therapeutic practice. I was, I believe, particularly daring – or perhaps foolhardy – in that book for I chose to describe a relationship with a woman who had come to see me because of grave sexual difficulties. Indeed, she herself collaborated with me in writing the chapter. I should like to end by quoting from the final section of the account where I am attempting to assess the significance of the relationship for my work as a therapist and for me as a person.

> In some ways, I have come to think that it was with Sally that I had the courage for the first time to test out the person-centred approach to the furthest limits. For more than a decade I had attempted to be accepting, empathic and genuine with my clients. I had also tried to trust their innate wisdom and to have faith in their capacity, given the right climate, to find their own way forward. Never before, however, had I found the courage and ability to experience and express those attitudes and beliefs so consistently over such a lengthy period of time.

With Sally I could not dodge the implications of believing that I am an eternal soul, that the source of all being is infinite love, that the body is the temple of the divine, that sexuality and spirituality are indivisible, that prayer is a route into the invisible world. To be genuine with Sally meant living out those beliefs in the moment-to-moment relationship with her. Talking about them was at times important and necessary, but far more fundamental was the way in which those beliefs coloured and permeated my acceptance, not only of her, but also of myself. I had to take my own soul and body seriously and to cherish them as much as I cherished hers . . . With Sally I dared to be whole because nothing less would do, and in the process I discovered levels of genuineness, acceptance and empathy that gave access to a transcendent world where healing occurs because the understanding is complete. In short, thanks to my work with Sally, I have come to acknowledge and to affirm that for me the practice of person-centred therapy cannot be divorced from my journey as an eternal soul . . .

I now believe that most existing theories of personality and personality development sell the human species short. With Sally, I came to recognise the essential mysteriousness of personality and found in this a refreshing change from theories which attempt to offer an almost complete understanding.

In summary, my work with Sally convinces me that, if two people believe that love is the governing power in the universe, and that we have not yet penetrated more than a fraction of the mystery of human personality or human relating, then they may be prepared to accept and to share their weakness, vulnerability, embarrassment and ineptitude and find that it is in the apparent poverty that riches are concealed. (Thorne, 1987: 65–7)

I have little doubt that my work with this client was the most taxing and the most rewarding I had undertaken up to that point in my career. What is more, I have never felt more responsible to someone nor more in touch with my own integrity. And yet I have a strange feeling that the courage that we both required had little to do with professional standards and responsibility as we usually understand them and very little to do with the letter of the ethical code and everything to do with its spirit. We were drawing pure water from the well of suffering, which is also the well of life. Could it be that this is the very water we are in danger of poisoning in our zeal to become exemplary professionals with impeccable credentials and ever-higher standards? The question does not go away.

References

Dryden W (ed.) (1987) Key Cases in Psychotherapy. London: Croom Helm.

Dryden W, Spurling L (eds) (1989) On Becoming a Psychotherapist. London: Tavistock/Routledge

Peck MS (1978) The Road Less Travelled. London: Hutchinson.

Thorne B (1987) Beyond the Core Conditions. In Dryden W (ed.) Key Cases in Psychotherapy. London: Croom Helm

Chapter 11
The Two Carls –
Reflections on Jung and
Rogers[1]

A personal indebtedness

It was in 1960 that I first discovered Carl Gustav Jung – and then by an indirect route. As a student at Cambridge I was studying the works of Hermann Hesse and began dimly to recognise that there was in Hesse a backdrop, a way of viewing reality and human nature which seemed to find hope even in the depth of despair, a kind of determined refusal to give in to the dark. Hesse was very aware, it seemed, of the presence of demonic forces and of the unsubdued animal in man. He showed evil relating to God but also subordinate to Him and serving His purposes in developing and transforming the self. It was my German supervisor at Cambridge – Elizabeth Stopp, Catholic and graphologist – who alerted me to the fact that Hesse had been a patient of Jung's and was deeply imbued with Jungian thought. Thus began my reading of Jung's works and an endless fascination with a man for whom the unconscious was not the gloomy ragbag that I had come to associate with the name of Freud but a source of hope and creativity. What is more Jung's concept of the collective unconscious permitted me to have a psychic ancestry in a way that seemed to bring into play a whole wealth of human experience beyond the boundaries of my own personal existence.

Carl Rogers entered my life some seven years later. His effect was different and highly practical. He provided me with the tools for deep self-acceptance and showed me what it might mean to love other people in a disciplined and consistent way. Jung showed me the breadth and depth and height of the human soul with its darkness and its light: Rogers gave me the means and the courage to relate to myself and others without passing judgement.

---

[1]This is part of a lecture originally given at the Norwich Centre and subsequently in the University of East Anglia in 1983.

I owe both Jung and Rogers a considerable personal debt and it is perhaps not surprising that such indebtedness has made me increasingly conscious over the years of many remarkable similarities between the two men. On the face of it this may seem surprising. Carl Jung was born in 1875 on the shores of Lake Constance, Switzerland, whereas Carl Rogers was born in 1902 at Oak Park near Chicago – the first a product of one of the most puritan and conservative countries in the world, the second a product of thrusting midwestern America. Today they personify for many people two schools of therapy that are often seen as significantly different in their understanding of human personality and development. At first sight, the two Carls may appear to have little in common except their fascination with the human psyche. The indisputable fact, however, is that they are remarkably similar in many respects.

There comes a moment, for example, in Carl Rogers' paper 'Empathic, an unappreciated way of being' when he says:

> Sensitive understanding by another may have been the most potent element in bringing the schizophrenic out of his estrangement, and into the world of relatedness. Jung has said that the schizophrenic ceases to be schizophrenic when he meets someone by whom he feels understood. Our study provides empirical evidence in support of that statement. (Rogers, 1975, p. 8)

Time and again there are echoes and reverberations of Jung in Rogers and of Rogers in Jung. Rogers' pride at producing empirical evidence in support of a statement by Jung is in itself revealing. Rogers presents himself as the rigorous scientist who is nonetheless deeply concerned with the complex and subjective experiences of the person labelled schizophrenic – a label that Jung, in his turn, deems superfluous once understanding is experienced. The worlds of objective and subjective knowledge intermingle and it is in this intermingling that the two Carls reveal their close kinship. Both men have enormous respect for the empirical approach to experience. They see themselves as hard headed and Rogers particularly has expended years of energy on detailed and thorough research of therapeutic processes. Jung, at the time of his break with Freud, while praising Freud as an empiricist of deep integrity, nonetheless accused him of being in possession of incomplete data about the nature of libido. The two men believe themselves to be dedicated empiricists who demand hard clinical evidence before they will advance theoretical hypotheses. What is more they both declare themselves to be continually open to new discoveries even if such discoveries threaten to throw their previous beliefs into disarray. And yet, for all their empiricism, both Carls showed a total commitment to the exploration of subjective experience and did so initially despite their growing awareness that such a commitment placed their own sanity in jeopardy.

This deep sense of vocation in both men produced a level of fearlessness that can only be described as heroic. The fields of battle that they chose were different but the same spirit was at work. Both are driven by an overwhelming urge to understand the nature of human experience and they are never satisfied with someone else's theories or perception. They wish to learn experientially and the raw material lies in their own lives and in the lives of those with whom they are closely in contact. It follows, therefore, that for them existence is without savour unless it is lived in depth for it is in the depth that the secrets of all hearts are revealed. If they sometimes appear to be iconoclasts or thorns in the sides of authority this is because both knew only too well how dogma, prejudice and fixed ideas can alienate a man or woman from their own thoughts and feelings so that in the end they cease to be human beings and become mere mouthpieces of religious or political credos. 'To thine own self be true' is a formidable motto: both Jung and Rogers held to it whatever the cost. In their different ways they have encouraged me, however imperfectly and faint-heartedly, to do the same.

The hero of the unconscious

Jung is the hero of the unconscious; Rogers is the hero of the intimate relationship. Both suffered to the point of breakdown in their quest for greater enlightenment. It was before the First World War that Carl Jung felt an irresistible urge and need to confront the depths of his own unconscious. At first he tried to do so by a detailed and scrupulous exploration of his childhood and adolescent memories but such a conscious approach, twice repeated, stood little chance of crossing the frontiers into the unknown. In torment, Jung was confronted by his own ignorance – and for him ignorance was the very hallmark of hell. His great intellect was of no avail. He was forced to stop thinking and simply to do what occurred to him. He submitted himself to the impulses of the unconscious in childlike trust. To those who were near to him at that time he must have seemed a childish fool, whose mental instability became increasingly apparent. He began to collect stones in his garden and to construct a model village. People could see him from the Lake of Zürich and must have wondered what the distinguished therapist was up to. He himself was partly delighted and partly ashamed but he had no option other than to follow his apparently mad impulses. Soon he was flooded by fantasies and caught up in shattering dreams. He was convinced that he was on the verge of psychosis and, typically, resolved to keep notes on his condition to the last possible moment so that he might leave something of value to posterity. He fell into uncontrollable rages and outbursts of frenzied weeping. His wife despaired of him and struggled to keep him sane in a house where his mistress, the young Toni Wolff, was often present as his *femme inspiratrice*. This extraordinary period persisted from 12 December 1913, when Jung in his own words 'plunged down into dark depths', until early 1916. Jung recalled later that he often had to keep repeating to himself 'I have a medical diploma from a Swiss university . . . I have a wife and five children. I live at 228 Seestrasse, Kusnacht' in order to find some reassurance. Remarkably enough he somehow managed to go on seeing patients although he did resign his lectureship at the University of Zürich because he felt it unfair to continue teaching students when his own intellectual situation was nothing but a mass of doubts.

It was in the midst of this torment and chaos that Jung discovered the raw material for the rest of his life's work. The anima, the collective unconscious, the archetype of the Self, the essential trustworthiness of the dark side – all these were glimpsed for the first time during those years of intense pain. Jung himself could write later that the years when he was pursuing his inner images were the most important in his life – in them everything essential was decided. He claimed that it all began then and that the later details were only supplements and clarifications of the material that burst forth from the unconscious, and at first swamped him. It was the fundamental material for his lifetime's work. There are, of course, other ways of looking at what happened. Vincent Brome in his biography of Jung suggests possibilities:

> Slowly the reasonably 'normal', conventional faithful married man, believing in one form of God, had been revealed as a person with bisexual potential, committing adultery, unreconciled to the personal God of Christianity and capable of murdering his father at one remove. At another level had he also come face to face with the person, presented by some witnesses, who took his wife's devotion for granted, insisted on incorporating his mistress into the family and showed very little interest in his children? Seen in technical terms Jung was a cyclothymic personality who suffered a manic-depressive psychosis. (Brome, 1978, p. 168).

In slightly provocative fashion I should like to propose a more complex verdict:

> Carl Jung, the distinguished therapist and academic, chose in 1913 to pursue heroically his vocation as a seeker after inner under-standing. He put aside his intellectual capacities and scholarly brilliance and submitted himself like a child to the impulses of his inner nature. He was courageous and self-absorbed enough to step across the frontiers of conventional morality and dogmatic religion and to cause his wife and family untold pain. He submitted to passion in all its ecstasy and torment and allowed a young woman to show him the woman inside himself and to tame her. He

permitted himself to hear voices and to walk in his garden with the creatures as he supposed of his own fantasy. But then he discovered he could not have created them because they were of such a nature that they had no source in his own experience. He allowed himself to live in a world populated by Freud, Salome, Elijah, Philemon, God the Father, Emma his wife, Toni his mistress, and many others real and fantastic, and he talked with them. In this state of altered consciousness he explored territory till then uncharted by human beings and returned with the outline of a map that was to revolutionise the practice of analysis. While arguably psychotic, he continued to see a number of patients and appears to have worked effectively with them. When war broke out in 1914 he was in Edinburgh giving a lecture on 'The Importance of the Unconscious in Psychopathology'.

The hero of the intimate relationship

In 1949 Carl Rogers was Executive Secretary (his own chosen title) of the Chicago University Counseling Center. His reputation was already considerable. *Counseling and Psychotherapy* had been published seven years before and *Client-Centered Therapy* was only two years away. The concepts of acceptance and empathy were to the fore and seen as the therapist's chief tools for helping the client to accept and understand his or her own feelings. To his colleagues Carl was warm, accepting, the attentive listener, the conscientious scholar, the trusting delegator of responsibility. In short the perfect empathiser who could move around in other people's skins and feel at home there. But who was he? One of his colleagues of those days put it succinctly: 'He is one of the most important people in my life and I hardly know him' (a remark attributed to TM Tomlinson and quoted by Howard Kirschenbaum in his biography of Rogers).

This warm, accepting, empathic and yet aloof man was about to enter into his period of torment. He who was already famous for his emphasis on the quality of relationship between counsellor and client was to be imprisoned in a relationship that nearly destroyed him. He has never written at length about this fateful episode but his biographer, Howard Kirschenbaum, has pieced together a number of published and unpublished accounts and here is what occurred in Rogers' own words:

There was a deeply disturbed client with whom I worked fairly extensively at Ohio State, who later moved to Chicago area and renewed her therapeutic contacts with me. I see now that I handled her badly, vacillating between being warm and real with her, and then being more 'professional' and aloof when the depth of her psychotic disturbance threatened me. She began to take up a bigger part of my therapy time – two or three times a week. She would sometimes appear sitting on our doorstep. I felt trapped by this kind of dependence. She said she needed more warmth and more realness from me. I wanted her to like me though I didn't like her. This brought about the most intense hostility on her part (along with dependence and love) which completely pierced my defences. (Kirschenbaum, 1979, p. 192)

The situation grew worse and worse. Rogers became convinced he was going insane and when one night he went to the cinema and saw a bizarre film he thought seriously about the hallucinations he would have when he was locked up and how they would emanate from the film. And yet he still continued to see the woman until he was so emotionally raw and so hooked on the notion that he had to be of help that he was on the very verge of complete breakdown. Rogers takes up the tale again:

Suddenly this feeling became very urgent. I had to escape. I am everlastingly grateful to Dr Louis Cholden, the promising young psychiatrist who was working in the Counseling Center at that time, for his willingness to take over the client at an hour's notice. I invited him to lunch at the Faculty Club. I said I needed help and explained the situation. He said, 'All right, how about my seeing her next week?' I must have shown something then and he must have been fairly sharp, because he added 'Or isn't that soon enough?' I said 'Well, she's coming in this afternoon!' I was really in a panic state at that time. I pulled a desperate trick on her. Knowing that she wouldn't want to see anyone else of her own accord, I arranged to give some kind of signal to the secretary, when Dr Cholden should come into the office. He came in, I said a few words to introduce them and quickly left. She, within moments, burst into a full-blown psychosis, with many delusions and hallucinations. She started telling Cholden of how she was related to me in some way, there was some uncle in Wisconsin and so on. As for me, I went home and told Helen that I must get away, at once. We were on the road within an hour and stayed away two or three months on what we can now calmly refer to as our 'runaway trip'. (Kirschenbaum, 1979, p. 193)

On his return Rogers was approached by one of his own staff members, Oliver Bown, who had the courage to tell him that it was obvious he was in deep distress and needed help. Bown had the even greater courage to tell Rogers that he was in no way afraid of him and that he was willing to offer his therapeutic services if Rogers felt able to accept them. Rogers, in his own words, 'accepted in desperation and gradually worked through to a point where I could value myself, even like myself, and was much less fearful of receiving or giving love. My own therapy with my clients has become consistently and increasingly free and spontaneous ever since that time' (Kirschenbaum, 1979, p. 193)

These comments of Rogers deserve close attention. Here was the therapist who over the years had helped hundreds of clients to a level of self-acceptance from a position where they were deeply self-rejecting. And yet it is clear that at a deep level Rogers himself had not come to self-acceptance. The impossible relationship with the disturbed woman had revealed a man who did not consider himself loveable at all. He could imagine that people might like what he did but he had no concept of himself as loveable, acceptable and estimable at the core of his being. In fact, he later admitted that he felt that in reality he was inferior and simply putting on a big front of competence and human effectiveness.

Empirical pilgrims

When Carl Jung 'plunged down into the dark depths of the unconscious' in terror and yet with deliberate intent he was already well known as the therapist of the unconscious and internationally recognised as second only to Freud in the analytical movement. When Carl Rogers went into therapy with Oliver Bown in order to learn how to love himself and how to offer and receive love he was already famous as the therapist of the relationship where acceptance and empathy were the agents of healing. Am I suggesting, then, that up to those climactic points in their careers Jung and Rogers were in some sense charlatans, preaching what they could not practise for themselves in their own lives? Not at all. I am inclined rather to think of them both as pilgrims who had reached a point in their journeys where it was no longer possible to turn back. The dark night of the soul had to be faced. The prospect of breakdown had to be endured if there was to be the hope of breakthrough. Experience alone could provide the empirical evidence that was required and both men knew that they alone could be the experiencers whose evidence they would believe. There was nothing for it but to make an act of faith.

A pilgrim's act of faith and dark nights of the soul are expressions that we associate with John Bunyan and St John of the Cross rather than with eminent psychologists. Am I suggesting that we should be adding two twentieth century saints to the calendar, St Carl of Zürich and St Carl of La Jolla? In a sense, I am, for I believe that Jung and Rogers are two of the most remarkable religious and spiritual figures of our century and, what is more, they are both extraordinary evangelists whose respective messages have more perhaps to offer than Billy Graham, even if he does manage to pack football grounds to capacity. Carl Rogers' brother, Walter, significantly enough, once described both Carl and his mother as Billy Graham types.

Extracts from their private writings are revealing:

I have had lots of time to think this summer and I feel that I have
come much closer to God, though there are thousands of things
that still perplex and baffle me. [Rogers at age 18 in a private diary
entry quoted in Kirschenbaum 1979, p. 17.]

It is a tremendous relief to quit worrying about whether you
believe what you are supposed to believe, and begin actually
studying Christ to find out whether he is a personality worth
giving your life to. I know that for myself that method of approach
has led me to a far deeper and far more enthusiastic allegiance to
Him. [Rogers at age 20, on return from China in a letter to his
parents quoted in Kirschenbaum, 1979 , p. 25.]

What about the failure of Communion to affect me? Was that my
own failure? I had prepared for it in all earnestness and hoped for
an experience of grace and illumination and nothing had
happened – God had been absent. For God's sake I now found
myself cut off from the Church and from my father's and every-
body else's faith. [Jung; 1993, p. 70.]

If at first sight the Swiss boy of the 1880s and the American boy of the
early twentieth century had little in common there was, in fact, one
highly significant similarity. Both grew up in homes where the Christian
religion permeated almost every aspect of living. Jung's father was a
Protestant minister and Rogers' parents were so deeply devoted to a
fundamentalist brand of evangelical Christianity that family prayers were
said every day and the Bible was the reference book for every occasion –
as long as the correct interpretation was provided. And yet the experience of the two boys was very different. Two vignettes illustrate the
contrast.

Julia Rogers, Carl's mother, often conducted family prayers and she
was particularly fond of two biblical phrases that were therefore often
inflicted upon the assembled family: 'Come out from among them and
be ye separate.' 'All our righteousness is as filthy rags in Thy sight, O
Lord.'

Jung's father, the Revd Paul Jung, vicar of Klein Hüningen, had
religious doubts although he resolutely refused to acknowledge them
until late in life. He prepared Carl for his first communion. The boy was
vibrant with expectancy and fascinated – as he remained throughout his
life – by paradoxes. Not surprisingly, he was attracted by the idea of the
Trinity: how could a oneness be simultaneously a threeness? When his
father came to this subject he said, with shattering honesty but to Carl's

utter disillusionment, 'We come now to the Trinity, but we'll skip that for I really understand nothing of it myself' (Hannah, 1976, p. 51).

In these two vignettes we can, I believe, see the signposts to the spiritual pilgrimages on which Jung and Rogers were to embark. Both boys were intensely religious and both were profoundly unnourished and disturbed by the religion with which they were presented at home. And yet the effect of that religion went deep. Long before Paul Jung was able to acknowledge the fact to himself, his son was profoundly aware of his father's doubts and confusions and of the way in which the correct observance of the liturgy had become a sterile structure in which there was no life. For Carl Rogers, however much he knew intellectually in later life that self-acceptance was at the heart of creative living, the words of his mother 'All our righteousness is as filthy rags in Thy sight, O Lord,'continued to fill him with a conviction of unworthiness and unloveability and however much he might wish to establish an egalitarian relationship with clients there was still the injunction to 'Come out from among them and be separate' with its inference of superiority and apartness.

I have described Jung as the hero of the unconscious and Rogers as the hero of the intimate relationship. I want now to change my terminology. If we think of the two men as spiritual pilgrims then I believe we can see Jung as the pilgrim of the journey to the Self and Rogers as the pilgrim of the journey to the Other. And both, I believe, have found God at the end of their journeys. Indeed, Carl Jung said as much in the famous interview that he gave on BBC television to John Freeman in 1959. Freeman asked him whether he believed in God. Jung replied with compelling simplicity 'I don't believe, I know' (Hannah, 1976 , p. 124). Confronted by the appallingness of his father's doubts Jung had risked all in the search for God in the darkness of his own unconscious. No other way was possible for nothing else but his own discoveries could have convinced him. Rogers does not use the name of God for fear that such a name will recreate again a figure of judgement and condemnation who will fill men and women with a profound sense of their own unworthiness, which they will strive in vain to shake off or to conceal through the effort of doing good. He does believe, however, in the life-transforming effect of relationships where acceptance, empathy and genuineness are present. He believes, in short, that love works. And God, as the writer of the Epistle of John said long ago, is love.

Living the great commandments

The two great commandments of the Christian Church are reiterated at many church services. 'Thou shalt love the Lord thy God with all thy heart, with all thy soul, with all thy mind and with all thy strength. Thou shalt love thy neighbour as thyself.' It is my contention that in our own century the rapid development of consciousness and of knowledge has made it increasingly impossible for many people – especially those of great intellectual and moral integrity – to obey either of these great commandments. The God of the Church has become incredible and the command to love oneself (for love of neighbour is in proportion to love of self) utterly impossible in the light of the multitudinous complexes (a Jungian word), guilts and anxieties with which modern men and women seem increasingly beset. In such a context the messages of Jung and Rogers are of the utmost importance and they have within them the flickering hope of preserving the spirit of man into the dawning of a New Age.

Carl Jung looked to his father to show him God and he looked to the Church of which his father was a minister. When he found there nothing but sterility and unacknowledged doubt or confusion he ceased to look for God outside of himself. If God were to be found then the search must be inward. As he gave himself over to the unconscious, Jung risked his sanity and in a very real sense prepared himself for the sacrifice of his conscious hold on reality. As he talked with Philemon by the side of the Lake and submitted himself to the archaic powers of the collective unconscious, he did not know whether he was surrounded by demons or angels. As he slept with Toni and wrestled with Emma's pain, he did not know if he was serving love or hate. He refused to yield to the paradox but held on in faith. The archetype of the Self was, for him, the eventual assurance that God is and that men and women are temples of the divine. And in his search he gave to modern men and women a new route to the knowledge of God – infinitely costly and demanding but requiring no allegiance to external authority and no submission to doctrinal formulations which can find support in neither reason nor personal experience. God is within and those who seek him in the twentieth century have no option but to make the inner journey.

The letter that Carl Rogers wrote home as he returned from his momentous visit to China and which I quoted earlier caused little joy to his parents. They were horrified by such comments as 'It is a tremendous relief to quit worrying about whether you believe what you are supposed to believe.' His insistence on the importance of the relationship with Jesus was good evangelical stuff but the notion that this should be an experience independent of sound biblical exegesis along strict evangelical lines filled them with dismay. Rogers has often remarked that his five-month visit to China – he went as a delegate to an international conference sponsored by the YMCA – enabled him to separate from his parents cleanly and painlessly insofar as he returned a new person with his identity firmly established. And yet we have seen that this was not wholly true. Years later he was to discover that he was still in his own eyes a 'filthy rag' in the sight of the Lord. All his efforts to offer a therapeutic relationship to others had not enabled him to love himself and to rejoice in the nature of his own being. He had to begin on the hard road to self-acceptance, which involved receiving from others the unconditional acceptance and understanding that had been denied him by his parents and their judgemental God. To love one's neighbour as oneself is a hard commandment and, for twentieth century men and women, it means nothing less than the rigorous discipline of submitting to the mystery of the 'I–Thou' relationship in human terms and accepting the ecstatic and agonising challenge of learning to accept, understand and cling to the truth contained in the flow of experience that characterises all relating. For too long Christians have been exhorted to love but twentieth century men and women can no longer pretend to do what they do not know how to do. In the life and work of Carl Rogers they can discover a way to loving and being loved that cannot be simulated but demands intense discipline and then offers its moments of sublime joy. The pilgrim to the Self makes it possible for us to know God and the pilgrim to the Other shows us how to love our neighbour as ourselves. What is more, they are both evangelists and in the latter part of their lives neither rested from proclaiming their message. Carl Rogers in his eighties travelled the world bringing together men and women from widely differing cultures into temporary communities where they could learn to listen, to understand and to respect each other at the deepest level. Carl Jung, as an old man, wrote *The Undiscovered Self*, in which he addressed the peoples of a world which he saw heading for disaster. Both men began their professional lives in a consulting room with individuals but end with a love of humanity that makes them inordinately concerned about the fate of the world. And here again they show themselves to be the very embodiment of the prophet for the twentieth century for it will be the ultimate irony if as we move towards the God who dwells within and learn truly to love ourselves and each other we find that we have no earth left on which to dwell.

References

Brome V (1978) Jung, Man and Myth. London : Granada Publishing.
Hannah B (1976) Jung, His Life and Work. New York: Capricorn Books.
Jung CG (1958) The Undiscovered Self. London: Routledge & Kegan Paul.
Jung CG (1993) Memories, Dreams, Reflections. London: Fontana Press.
Kirschenbaum H (1979) On Becoming Carl Rogers. New York: Delacorte Press.
Rogers CR (1942) Counseling and Psychotherapy. Boston: Houghton Mifflin.
Rogers CR (1951) Client-Centered Therapy. Boston: Houghton Mifflin.
Rogers CR (1975) Empathic: an unappreciated way of being. The Counseling Psychologist 2: 2–10.

Chapter 12
Beyond the Consulting
Room[1]

A major difficulty in assessing Rogers' overall influence on counselling and psychotherapy is the fact that, unlike most other professional therapists, he was not content to remain in his consulting room. There are those who profoundly regret this and would much have preferred him to have stayed at the University of Chicago and to have continued in patient clinical practice and research until retirement, to the undoubted benefit of subsequent generations of therapists throughout the world. Instead he chose to move out into the untidy confusion of encounter groups, cross-cultural communication, peace work and what cynics regarded as a mission to convert the world to the person-centred approach. Some have never forgiven him for this apparent grandiosity of intent, and very recently one of his former students and associates, Dr Bill Coulson, hit the headlines by launching a full-scale attack on what he considers the grave error Rogers made of generalising from insights formulated in the counselling room to conclusions about how life should be lived in families, schools and society at large. Coulson currently appears on American radio and television and testifies before legislative committees on education, drug abuse and juvenile delinquency. He believes that both he and Rogers owe the nation's parents an apology for having so grievously misled them into thinking that their children should be offered the core conditions and encouraged to make up their own minds about the direction of their lives. So extreme has Coulson become in his denigration of the ideas of his former mentor, colleague and friend that he recently implied that Rogers repudiated his philosophy late in life and acknowledged that he was in error. Howard Kirschenbaum, Rogers' biographer, has felt obliged to answer Coulson and to dismiss as totally without foundation the suggestion that Rogers in any way repudiated his beliefs (Kirschenbaum, 1991). What is

[1]Originally published as part of Chapter 5 in Thorne B (1992) *Carl Rogers*. London: Sage Publications Ltd, and reprinted by permission of the publishers.

particularly interesting about this whole bizarre sequence of events is Coulson's apparent conviction that Rogers' ideas have had and are continuing to have such a powerful effect on people's lives. The passion and intensity of Coulson's campaign can only be explained by his belief that Rogers' ideas are transforming society and that the transformation is pernicious.

It is perhaps significant that Bill Coulson is a committed Roman Catholic and it appears that his current zeal is fired by the realisation that, for him, Rogers' ideas and beliefs had become a modern-day religious system. Interestingly, Coulson does not refute the basic tenets of client-centred therapy, which he still believes to be correct; his quarrel is with the application of discoveries made about psychotherapy to other areas of human life – notably education and the family unit. This particular crusade will doubtless run its course and soon be forgotten but the issues at the heart of the affair are, I believe, both fascinating and important.

As someone who has frequently facilitated person-centred encounter groups in many parts of the world and often been a member of cross-cultural communities, I am well aware of the transforming effects that such groups can have on many participants. There is a sense in which these experiences can lead to a greatly heightened sense of awareness and a much-enhanced feeling both of self-worth and of interconnected-ness with others. The encounter group can provide an avenue into a level of experiencing that can appropriately be described as spiritual, mystical, transcendental (Thorne, 1988, p. 201). Such experiences are naturally short-lived, but they touch people at the deepest level and often leave them both exhilarated and disturbed. For those who have no previous experience of such intensity and no religious or spiritual frame-work into which they can 'fit', what has happened to them, the under-pinning philosophy of Rogers' work, becomes their credo. What they have experienced is of a spiritual order so it is understandable that they should elevate Rogers' ideas and the person-centred 'movement' to the same level. Rogers' ideas then become all-embracing and affect every aspect of their lives – and that, for Bill Coulson, is where the trouble begins.

Coulson's current perturbation was foreshadowed by Paul Vitz in his book *Psychology as a Religion,* which appeared in 1977. Vitz argues persuasively that the most direct source for what he describes as contem-porary 'humanistic selfism' is Ludwig Feuerbach's *The Essence of Christianity,* which first appeared in 1841. The book was an influential attack on Christianity in so far as Feuerbach postulated that God is merely the projected essence of man and that the highest law of ethics is that man's selfless love for humanity constitutes salvation. Feuerbach argued that what was formerly viewed and worshipped as God is now recognised as something human. Man becomes man's God. Feuerbach, in Vitz's estimation, directly or indirectly affected the thinking of Marx,

Nietzsche, Huxley, John Stuart Mill and – most significantly – Freud and Dewey. Rogers fits neatly at the end of this line of descent as the disciple of Dewey through the mediation of William Heard Kilpatrick.

Vitz is not content with citing Rogers' essentially anti-Christian precursors. He discovers that in the United States there were popular Protestant ministers during the period from 1920 to the mid-1950s who embraced such concepts as 'self-realisation', 'becoming a real person' and the primacy of *becoming* over *being* without abandoning the Christian church. In Vitz's eyes their Christianity was a strangely emasculated and superficial version of the true faith yet it is clear that their message had great appeal for many Americans who did not wish to jettison a religious view of reality. Vitz quotes, in particular, the work of Harry Emerson Fosdick and Norman Vincent Peale and draws somewhat ironical attention to the fact that Fosdick's *On Being a Real Person* (1943) preceded Rogers' *On Becoming a Person* by almost 20 years. Both Fosdick and Peale were deeply involved in pastoral counselling and drew extensively on contemporary psychological insights. Vitz notes that, for Fosdick, integration and self-realisation replaced the theological concept of salvation. In Vitz's view the period of Fosdick and Peale was one of transition, which responded to the needs of a population disenchanted with basic Christian theology and ignorant of real spirituality but still unwilling to relinquish a religious framework. The post World War II generation, however, was ready for a humanistic selfism that had finally lost the trappings of the diluted Christianity of their parents' generation. The time was ripe for humanistic psychology to come into its own and Carl Rogers was to become the acknowledged leader not only of a psychological 'third force' to challenge the ascendancy of analysis and behaviourism but also, in Vitz's eyes, of an applied philosophy that amounted to a new secular religion (Vitz, 1977, p. 66–82).

Vitz and other writers find further historical precedents for Rogers' later work with encounter groups and large communities in the Christian pietism and Jewish Hasidism of the eighteenth and nineteenth centuries. More recently, in a paper presented at Stirling University, Louise Yeoman of St Andrew's University, Scotland, also discovers unlikely parallels with person-centred therapy in the experience of seventeenth century Calvinists (Yeoman, 1991). Fascinating as these similarities are, their chief relevance in attempting to assess Rogers' overall influence lies in the fact that experiences of personal growth and interpersonal intimacy akin to those recorded by participants in person-centred contexts have in the past commonly been associated with the religious and spiritual understanding of reality. It is scarcely surprising that at the present time the process seems to be operating in the reverse direction: the 'secular' experience of person-centred groups in particular seems for some people to open up a channel into spiritual terrain that has previously remained unexplored and whose very existence has been denied.

It is my own conviction that Rogers' early experiences, however perverse the theology underpinning them, ensured that his understanding of subjective phenomena and of interpersonal relationships could not in the end fail to embrace what, in his own words, he described as the transcendent, the indescribable, the spiritual. For Coulson and for Vitz such language is presumably a sinister indication of the grandiosity of a psychotherapeutic approach that aspires to become a philosophy of life or, even worse, a substitute religion. Both condemn Rogers as hostile to true religion and particularly to Christianity and see his ideas as destructive of family life and detrimental to the creation of a responsible society. Vitz, indeed, places Rogers at the end of a line of thinkers who have consistently undermined Christianity since the nineteenth century. My own perception is radically different. Paradoxically, the vehemence of the attack on Rogers by such Christian apologists as Vitz and Coulson serves to reinforce my conviction that Rogers' deep ambivalence towards institutional religion is an inevitable outcome not only of his own negative experience of a constraining theology but also of his openness to experience and thus to spiritual reality. The evidence, I believe, is overwhelming that Rogers, in his deep respect for human beings and in his trust of the actualising tendency, has enabled many to discover that at the deepest centre of the person and infusing the organismic self is the human spirit which is open to the transcendent. This discovery, which is the very essence of spirituality, often results in a move towards a belief in God and in the divine quality inherent in men and women that would previously have been inconceivable for those who thus find themselves unexpectedly launched on a spiritual journey. Fifty years from now it is likely that Rogers will be remembered not so much as the founder of a new school of psychotherapy but as a psychologist whose work made it possible for men and women to apprehend spiritual reality at a time when conventional religion had lost its power to capture the minds and imaginations of the vast majority. The spiritual thread in Rogers' work that remained covert and even denied for most of his professional life eventually emerges not as a mysterious dimension but as the outcome of faith in the actualising tendency and in the power of the core conditions to bring about transformation. When Rogers spoke in 1986 of inner spirit touching inner spirit and of a therapeutic relationship transcending itself and becoming 'part of something larger' he was not deserting the 'third force' of humanistic psychology and throwing in his lot with the 'fourth force' of the transpersonal psychologists. Rogers did not set out in any conscious and deliberate way to give his 'presence' to clients and thus to sweep them up into a new spiritual reality. This fourth quality, however it is defined, was simply the outcome of his trust in the client's actualising tendency and his commitment to the offering of the core conditions. And yet – as he discovered, and with him countless others whether therapists or clients, facilitators or members of encounter groups – the effect is totally transforming for it enables transcendence to occur so that a new perspective can be achieved. As I have written elsewhere:

> Always there is a sense of well-being, of it being good to be alive and this in spite of the fact that problems or difficulties which confront the client remain apparently unchanged and as intractable as ever. Life is good and life is impossible, long live life. (Thorne, 1985, p. 10)

Thoroughgoing phenomenologist that he was, Rogers never attempted to impose his version of reality on anyone else, and the same remains true when we speak of a spiritual or transcendent reality. In a remarkable article written in 1978, 'Do we need "a" reality?' Rogers concluded:

> I, and many others, have come to a new realisation. It is this: The only reality I can possibly know is the world as I perceive and experience it at this moment. The only reality you can possibly know is the world as you perceive and experience it as this moment. And the only certainty is that those perceived realities are different. There are as many 'real worlds' as there are people! This creates a most burdensome dilemma, one never before experienced in history. (Rogers, 1978, p. 7)

It is nonetheless this 'burdensome dilemma' that Rogers' work enables us to shoulder and through it to discover freedom in transcendence. The spiritual world to which the person-centred approach often gives access is not caught up in dogmatic formulations or ethical certainties for it, too, has as many facets as there are people who experience it.

Rogers dreamed of a world where society was based on the hypothesis of multiple realities and believed that such a society would not be characterised by selfishness and anarchy. He had a vision of a community of persons no longer motivated by a blind commitment to a cause or creed or view of reality, but by a common commitment to each other as separate persons with their own separate realities. As he put it: 'The natural human tendency to care for another would no longer be "I care for you because you are the same as I" but, instead, "I prize and treasure you because you are different from me"' (Rogers, 1978, p. 9).

The most far-reaching of Rogers' many contributions may well turn out to be this assurance that in order to affirm our natures we do not have to put on the straitjacket of a common creed or shared dogma but can celebrate the mysterious paradox of our uniqueness and our membership one of another.

References

Fosdick HE (1943) On Being a Real Person. New York: Harper.

Kirschenbaum H (1991) Denigrating Carl Rogers: William Coulson's last crusade. Journal of Counseling and Development 69: 411–13.

Rogers CR (1961) On Becoming a Person. Boston: Houghton Mifflin.

Rogers CR (1978) Do we need 'a' reality? Dawnpoint 1(2): 6–9.

Thorne BJ (1985) The Quality of Tenderness. Norwich: Norwich Centre Publications.

Thorne BJ (1988) The person-centred approach to large groups. In M Aveline and W Dryden (eds) Group Therapy in Britain. Milton Keynes: Open University Press, pp. 185–207.

Vitz P (1977) Psychology as Religion: the Cult of Self-Worship. Grand Rapids MI: William B Eerdmans.

Yeoman L (1991) 'Calvinism, conversion and the person-centred approach'. Unpublished presentation at the Second International Conference on Client-Centred and Experiential Psychotherapy, University of Stirling, Scotland.

Chapter 13
Spirituality and the
Counsellor[1]

I am an atheist and find the whole area of spirituality in counselling confusing. My problem lies in the vague, wishy-washy ways in which people discuss this topic. I want to understand it better, so can you give me a brief description of spirituality in counselling and its value for a confused atheist?

I am not surprised that you find the area of spirituality confusing and I can imagine that, as an atheist, you must be somewhat daunted by the recent upsurge of interest in this area throughout the whole counselling world. Perhaps it is important therefore at the outset to separate the notion of spirituality from a belief structure that posits the existence of God or an elaborated system of religious dogma. As far as the counsellor is concerned, spirituality has relevance primarily because it concerns the nature of the self and the relationship between counsellor and client.

There have been many attempts to formulate theories of the self ranging from complex maps of the unconscious to a view of human nature based on biological drives or behaviourally conditioned reflexes. Every counsellor will have his or her own working concept of the self whether this is fully conscious and articulated or not. For the counsellor or client who takes the spiritual dimension seriously, however, this concept of the self, whether it incorporates, for example, the power of the unconscious, the need for unconditional love or even the influence of intra-uterine experience, will affirm that the ultimate foundation of our being is spiritual and that it is in the spiritual dimension that the true source of who we are is to be found.

The implications of this view of human nature are profound. Sadly, however, as John Rowan amongst others has shown (Rowan, 1990) one

[1]Originally published in 1993 as Chapter 14 in *Questions and Answers on Counselling in Action* (ed. W Dryden). London: Sage Publications Ltd, and reprinted by permission of the publishers.

of the great problems around spirituality is that it is highly resistant to language. This may well be why you find yourself complaining about the 'vague, wishy-washy ways' in which the subject is often discussed. The reason for this resistance to language lies in the fact that spirituality goes beyond psychology and beyond any discipline that relies principally on language for its expression and is limited to it. Nonetheless if I hold to a concept of the self (as I do) that affirms spirit to be the fundamental ingredient, then it is incumbent upon me to do battle with language, however resistant. For me the individual's spirit or spiritual dimension is his or her creative source of energy, which reflects the moving force within the universe itself. In other words, it is because I am essentially a spiritual being that I am, whether I know it or not or whether I like it or not, indissolubly linked to all that is or has been or will be. I am not an isolated entity but rather a unique part of the whole created order. What is more, this spiritual essence of my being defines me in a way that goes far beyond my genetic inheritance, my conditioning and all the ramifications of my unconscious processes. Furthermore, although at the present time my spiritual being manifests itself in the material form of my corporeal existence, it is not limited to that form. As Jill Hall has succinctly expressed it, 'Matter cannot be without spirit and is thus indivisible from spirit, although spirit can be without matter' (Hall, 1990). Spirit itself, unlike matter, is not subject to destruction, which means that my fundamental self transcends the boundaries of time and space.

It may be that this attempt on my part to find language to express the spiritual nature of the self has left you more confused than ever. Let me come at the subject from a different angle. I would suggest that from time to time most of us are struck by extraordinary coincidences or we have sudden premonitions or we may be overwhelmed by powerful feelings of love or of oneness. If we are less fortunate, we get caught up in fearful anxieties or we sense the appalling power of evil or we are unaccountably plunged into the most unimaginable despair. At the time such experiences feel very real and they may affect us profoundly but frequently we fail to integrate them into our concept of reality and we do not see their relevance to an understanding of our own natures. They are likely to remain as 'coincidences' or 'feelings which come over me' or 'peak experiences' or 'waking nightmares'. We are less likely to say to ourselves that we have entered a world infinitely more extensive and astonishing than the work-a-day reality to which we are normally confined. In short, we may fail to acknowledge that, because we are spiritual beings, we have access to levels of experiencing which transcend by far the narrow boundaries of our rational world.

How on earth could all this be of use to you, as an atheist, in your work as a counsellor? In the first place, it might encourage you to entertain a different concept of your own nature and that of your client.

Second, it might help you to accompany more effectively those clients for whom their spirituality is a basic assumption. Most importantly, however, it might make you less anxious as a counsellor and enable you to tap into resources that, at the moment, are perhaps denied you because you cannot credit their existence. Let me explain this last remark by reference to my own experience. For me, apart from certain fundamental and transforming experiences that I had as a young boy, my confrontation with the spiritual dimension of my own being has come about principally through the exercise of my profession as a counsellor. Frequently – and increasingly in recent years – both in individual and group counselling, I have been privileged to experience what I call 'magic moments'. Often such moments are the signal for a particular intensity of relating in which a new level of understanding is achieved and a powerful sense of validation by both client and counsellor. Outwardly situations may remain unchanged and the client's predicament, for example, may seem as intractable as ever. And yet, everything is different because a new creative energy has been tapped into which could variously be described as the power of love, the spirit of hope or the sense of ultimate security. Sometimes such 'magic moments' lead to an acceptance of powerlessness on my part, an acceptance that is not a sign of resignation, a kind of 'I give up' syndrome but rather something that unites counsellor and client and leads to a waiting without expectation but also without despair.

I believe that such acceptance of powerlessness is rare in our culture. We tend to want solutions and to expect an answer to every problem (often to be provided by an expert). We become frustrated and angry when no solution seems to be available. The acceptance of powerlessness of which I speak, however, is a recognition of our own limitations and at the same time an acknowledgement of the infinite resources by which we are surrounded. In such a context I find as the counsellor that I am no longer anxious to prove myself to be the 'good' therapist who has to provide all the right answers or facilitate all the right developments. What is more the client, too, can relax into not knowing without being frightened or frustrated. I have come to regard this acceptance of powerlessness as one of the major fruits of trusting in the spiritual foundation of the created order and of human nature. It leads to a waiting upon the spirit which is almost always creative and which frequently leads to unexpected outcomes. Such waiting seems to transcend normal time boundaries and has the powerful effect of removing anxiety about the future. In short, counsellor and client experience their place in the spiritual order and live, even if only briefly, in the light of eternity. At such moments living in the present becomes not only desirable but easy.

A final challenge, if you are by now almost persuaded that I am not completely off my head. When you are next stuck in your work with a client, acknowledge your stuckness and invite your client to join you in waiting without anxiety for the process to unfold. If you genuinely care for your client and if he or she knows that you care, you may well be astonished by what follows. You will also know something about what many of your colleagues call spirituality even if you choose never to employ the word.

References

Hall J (1990) Transformation in counselling. British Journal of Guidance and Counselling 18(3): 269–80.
Rowan J (1990) Spiritual experiences in counselling. British Journal of Guidance and Counselling 18(3): 233–49.

Chapter 14
Body and Spirit[1]

I have read your case in Windy Dryden's *book entitled* Key Cases in Psychotherapy *where you describe your work with a client, which culminated in a nude embrace between the two of you. While I understand the context in which this happened and the therapeutic value it had for your actions, you were in breach of the BAC Code of Ethics and Practice with respect to counsellors not engaging in sexual activity with their clients. Can you comment on this?*

I am aware that before I can have any hope of responding to your question there is a need to fill in the background. Let me acknowledge from the outset that the description of my 'key case' in Windy Dryden's edited book has been the cause of more comment, correspondence and general discussion than almost anything else I have ever written and there are times when I wish I had been more cowardly (or less foolhardy) and never set pen to paper (Thorne, 1987). Having said that, I welcome this opportunity to revisit the terrain that my client, Sally, and I explored together and to attempt to throw more light on some of the issues involved. It is perhaps worth noting, incidentally, that almost all the correspondence I have received about this notorious chapter has been overwhelmingly positive. One further point which needs to be noted is that the work with Sally took place between 1979 and 1983, that is before the 1984 BAC Code of Ethics first prohibited sexual activity with clients. I could not in any case have been in breach of something that, at that time, did not exist.

Despite my occasional fantasy that the whole country knows about my relationship with Sally in detail, I am modest enough to assume that most of the readers of this book will know nothing of it whatsoever.

---

[1]Originally published as Chapter 22 in *Questions and Answers on Counselling in Action* (ed W Dryden). London: Sage Publications Ltd (1993). Reprinted by permission of the publishers.

Briefly, then, Sally was a married client with grave sexual problems with whom I worked for a period of some three years at the beginning of the 1980s. She was the wife of a priest and the couple originally came to see me together after many years of ineffective marital therapy with other practitioners including psychiatrists. They had chosen me because they already knew me socially, had read much of my published work and, most importantly, because I shared their Christian perception of reality. Although Sally quickly came into individual therapy with me, her husband, Kenneth, was kept fully informed of our work throughout its process and both he and the couple's children were actively involved at certain crucial stages. When the 'key case' came to be written up both Sally and Kenneth were fully involved in its composition.

As I explain in the chapter itself, my work with Sally took me into uncharted territory and I am still, 10 years later, awe-struck by the extra-ordinary nature of our therapeutic journey. Without doubt it was a milestone in my personal and professional development and my work since owes much to the discoveries made at that time. Most relevant to your question is the fact that during the course of therapy Sally discovered that she had no option but to allow herself to regress to earlier experience and ultimately to intra-uterine pain. What is more, despite initial shame and terror, she chose to do some of this work either partially or completely unclothed while seeking my co-operation in holding her and, on occasion, in applying gentle massage to various parts of her body. Clearly such work was only undertaken after the most careful review of its implications and, indeed, after a referral to a female therapist trained in body work (which I am not) who was wise enough to see that she could not exonerate me from undertaking a task that belonged to the relationship between Sally and me and could not conveniently be transferred elsewhere.

You will know from your reading of the 'key case' that Sally was (and is) a beautiful woman and that I understandably experienced sexual feelings towards her. My dilemma was whether these feelings could be put at the service of the therapeutic work and thus integrated into my response to her in such a way that she could experience my integrity and thus be encouraged to trust her own. It was here that our shared Christian understanding and the involvement of her husband were so crucial. It rapidly became apparent that if I was to be of real use to Sally I needed to have the deepest possible love for her as a person and to be free to exercise that love in the service of her healing. Essentially, then, my work with Sally became a matter of soul loving because both she and I (and Kenneth) believed that the deepest part of the person is the indwelling spirit or soul where God is to be found. But to love Sally as an immortal soul meant a total willingness to accept her as an incarnate being in all her emotionality, physicality and sexuality. What is more, this could only be done if I could be confident that my own sexuality was sufficiently integrated within my own being that there was no danger of my abusing Sally or Kenneth or my own wife by moving across boundaries into a relationship where sexuality assumed the primacy. Without doubt there was a risk involved in all this but I would submit that there are few therapeutic relationships of depth where risks are not involved. In this instance our shared Christian allegiance, the involvement of Kenneth and the deepening sense of mutuality between us were, I believe, more than adequate safeguards.

It is within this overall context that the incident of the naked embrace referred to in your question has to be considered. It should be remembered, too, that this event occurred very near the end of therapy and at a stage where a deep mutuality had existed between us for some time. For Sally the moment was critical; for perhaps the first time she was experiencing the full flow of her sexual and creative energy and she was terrified that she would not be able to control it. What is more, she feared she would be destroyed by it and do much evil in the process. My behaviour – and the original text indicates the immense tension I experienced within me during those few moments – was a direct response to her overwhelming fear both of fragmentation and of corruption. By risking my own naked vulnerability and trusting my own integrity I hoped to convey to Sally that she need not fear her sexuality and that her ethical self, based as it was on a deep love of souls, would ensure that her sexuality would confirm her loving rather than corrupt it into lust. It is perhaps not unimportant that I was proved right.

My direct response, therefore, to your question is that in my naked embrace of Sally I was not engaging in sexual activity. For me to do so in a relationship is to seek pleasure in sexual behaviour or to incite the other to seek such pleasure; it involves a deliberate attempt to engage in activity which will arouse sexual feelings in oneself or the other so that these feelings can subsequently be consummated through intercourse or other forms of sexual satisfaction. My naked embrace of Sally was in many ways the antithesis of such behaviour. As a statement it conveyed the message:

> It is possible for a man and woman who love each other and who are attracted to each other sexually to be naked and vulnerable together without self-betrayal and without betraying others. What is more such vulnerability by challenging the tyrannical primacy of sexual desire can hasten integration and spiritual growth.

In the last analysis, I suppose, the credibility of my answer to your question depends to a large extent on whether or not you accept the belief that, at the deepest level, we are spiritual beings and that our greatest need is for spiritual development. If such a view is unacceptable to you I can imagine that, despite your generous acknowledgement that my behaviour with Sally had therapeutic value for her, you may well still conclude that entering into a naked embrace with her was essentially a sexual activity. All my talk of integration and spiritual growth will perhaps seem to you little more than an elaborate form of self-deception and you will be left with the problem of determining whether I am a benevolent or malevolent self-deceiver. I am aware, incidentally, that the current interpretation of the BAC Code leaves me in one or other of these categories, but I should, of course, wish to challenge strongly that interpretation.

It is of some reassurance to me to know that others more eminent that I have struggled with many of the issues by which I was confronted in my relationship with Sally. In his best-selling book *The Road Less Travelled,* the American psychiatrist Scott Peck has this to say:

> Because of the necessarily long and intimate nature of the psychotherapeutic relationship, it is inevitable that both patients and therapists routinely develop strong or extremely strong sexual attractions to each other. The pressures to sexually consummate such attractions may be enormous. I suspect that some of those in the profession of psychotherapy who cast stones at a therapist who has related sexually with a patient may not themselves be loving therapists and may not therefore have any real under-standing of the enormity of the pressures involved. Moreover, were I ever to have a case in which I concluded after careful and judicious consideration that my patient's spiritual growth would be substantially furthered by our having sexual relations, I would proceed to have them. In fifteen years of practice, however, I have not yet had such a case, and I find it difficult to imagine that such a case could really exist. (Peck, 1979, pp. 175–6)

My own position mirrors Peck's statement almost exactly and it is inter-esting to note that since writing *The Road Less Travelled* Peck has himself embraced a Christian commitment and presumably now has as much trouble with church attitudes to sexuality as I do. The criterion of the client's spiritual growth remains for me the ultimate and overwhelm-ingly important issue in the monitoring of my own behaviour as a counsellor. When I took the risk of holding Sally in a naked embrace it was because I believed that in doing so I might enable her spiritual growth to be 'substantially furthered'. For me it was not 'engaging in sexual activity' but a perilous leap of faith undertaken on behalf of a human soul who had shown me such trust that I could be nothing less for her than my total self.

References

Peck MS (1979) The Road Less Travelled. A New Psychology of Love, Traditional Values and Spiritual Growth. New York: Simon and Schuster.

Thorne BJ (1987) Beyond the core conditions. In W Dryden (ed.) Key Cases in Psychotherapy. London: Croom Helm.

Chapter 15
Developing a Spiritual
Discipline[1]

> *I am compelled to believe that I, like many others, have underes-*
> *timated the importance of this mystical, spiritual dimension.*
> (Rogers, 1980, p. 130)

Among the 'post-Rogerians' there is something of a battle raging about
the importance of Rogers' claims in the final decade of his life to have
discovered a new and powerful dimension in the therapeutic relationship. In short, he believed that when he was functioning at his best and
therefore offering the core conditions with maximum effectiveness,
something qualitatively different could happen. He described this as the
experience of discovering that simply his presence was releasing and
helpful. 'At those moments', he wrote, 'it seems that my inner spirit has
reached out and touched the inner spirit of the other. Our relationship
transcends itself and becomes a part of something larger. Profound
growth and healing and energy are present' (Rogers, 1980: 129). In the
face of these startling assertions many person-centred practitioners tend
to be embarrassed or even dismissive. There are certainly those who
state, either publicly or privately, that such wildly grandiose claims are
attributable to Rogers' declining faculties or to a kind of *folie de*
grandeur which sometimes afflicts great men as they approach death.

I find myself in a different camp from these detractors. Unlike them I
am excited by Rogers' attempt to articulate his experience of the
mystical. When he speaks of the 'transcendental core' of his being I find
no conflict between this concept and the notion of the 'actualising
tendency' that underpins the person-centred understanding of personality and therapeutic process. My ready endorsement of Rogers' claims
springs from my own experience of precisely the phenomena that he
describes. What is more, I believe that, as a person-centred counsellor, I

---

[1]Originally published in 1994 as Chapter 12 in *Developing Person-Centred Counselling*, D
Mearns. London: Sage Publications Ltd. Reprinted by permission of the publishers.

have a responsibility to attend to my own being and to the relationship with my clients in such a way that this quality of presence with its remarkable capacity for promoting growth, healing and energy is more likely to be experienced. Clearly, as Rogers himself states, nothing can be done to force such an outcome within the course of a therapeutic encounter and the thought of setting out deliberately and consciously to create the experience of presence is preposterous. The issue is more subtle and complex; it involves the willingness of the therapist to live out consistently and profoundly the philosophy that the person-centred approach embraces. More particularly it requires the disciplined practices of self-exploration and self-acceptance and of the focused holding of the absent client. It is my belief – and experience – that a commitment to such a discipline on the part of the counsellor greatly increases the likelihood of therapeutic relationships where the transcendental core of client and counsellor can be brought together with a resulting release of healing energy.

In my own life the practice of self-exploration and self-acceptance comprises a number of different elements and I shall discuss these briefly in a moment. I am sure, however, that each practitioner must discover for himself or herself the practice with which he or she feels most comfortable. There can be no blueprint that is universally applicable. It goes without saying, too, that the discipline I am describing supplements and greatly extends the benefits of the traditional supervision relationship but in no way replaces it. The discipline I have worked out for myself has five elements and involves a consideration of my current response to various aspects of my experiencing. The task in each case is to conduct an exploration and to arrive, if at all possible, at a position where I am able to accept myself for what I am. The discipline lends itself to a variety of settings – to periods alone in my study, to the walk home after a long day in the counselling room, to a journey by train. What matters for me is that it should be done systematically and regularly. The first element concerns my relationship with my body. I reflect on my thoughts and feelings about my physical being and try to face those areas where I am self-rejecting or self-deprecatory. I attempt to be as compassionately disposed towards my body as possible and ask myself how I am treating it through what I eat and drink, through the clothes I wear, through the rest I give it and the activities I pursue. Where it seems I am lacking in compassion I resolve to become more caring of the body, which has the awesome task of carrying me through the world. The second element concerns my relationship with others and here I deliberately exclude my clients (they have their turn later!). I ask myself how cherished I feel and how cherishing in turn I am to others. Sometimes I discover that I am making do on starvation rations. I am not putting myself in the way of love and appreciation and I am even failing to smile at the postman. Self-acceptance is scarcely nurtured by such closedness and I want to open myself again to loving and being loved. The third element focuses on my use of time. I ask myself what I am doing in my work and with my leisure. Whatever I discover, I am resolved to move to a position where I can feel as accepting as possible of the time structures in which I find myself and of the activities to which I am committed. The fourth element concerns my awareness of the created order of which I am a part. By this I do not mean simply the natural environment of trees, flowers, animals, sun and rain but also the creations of humankind – buildings, works of art, music, poetry, beauty in all its forms. Reflection on this element sometimes reduces me to tears when I am forced to acknowledge that I have not read a poem for a month or allowed my eyes to linger on a tree all week. Such deprivation is a sign of self-neglect rather than self-acceptance. Finally, and most important of all, I put myself in the presence of my God. If I were an atheist or a humanist I would, I suspect, give myself over to the meaning of my life or to whatever higher power or influence irradiated my destiny. This is an exercise in total surrender so that I am immersed in God and allow myself to experience my unique and absolute value without hindrance or self-recrimination.

The discipline I have so far described has as its sole objective the cultivation and the maintenance of a loving disposition towards myself. The self-acceptance of the person-centred counsellor is a necessary cornerstone of person-centred practice and it is my contention that a discipline of this kind, regularly and systematically practised, leads to an enduring self-love that releases the counsellor from all self-preoccupation and greatly increases the possibility of a transcendental encounter with clients that is powerfully healing and releasing. There is, however, a second practice that, I believe, further increases the likelihood of such an encounter and this I call holding the absent client.

Many clients complain that they find it difficult to believe that their counsellors care about or even think about them between sessions. For some, the sense of abandonment and the agony of separation are weekly occurrences. Clearly, however, it is unhealthy for any counsellor to become so preoccupied with a client that his or her inner life becomes disrupted by such concern. Nonetheless, in my experience, it is powerfully enhancing of the relationship if the counsellor holds his or her clients in mind on a daily basis. The discipline is simple: it consists of focusing on each client in turn, bringing him or her to mind and calling up a visual image of the person in question. The counsellor then holds the client in a metaphorical embrace of acceptance and understanding for a minute or two. I am convinced that such a discipline greatly strengthens the relationship between counsellor and client and taps into those very forces that become so powerfully operative in the transcendental encounter. The client need never know of the counsellor's daily discipline on his or her behalf although there are those who are profoundly aided by such knowledge of their counsellor's commitment to them.

Carl Rogers, in a later elaboration of the passage referred to at the beginning of this section, says of the person-centred approach that when it is lived 'it helps the person expand the development of his or her own capacities' (Rogers, 1986, p. 200). It has been my intention to suggest that person-centred counsellors, by the exercise of the discipline I have described, can so increase their capacities that their simple presence in a therapeutic relationship will be more likely to release the healing energies which become powerfully active when a relationship 'transcends itself and becomes part of something larger'.

References

Rogers CR (1980) A Way of Being. Boston: Houghton Mifflin.

Rogers CR (1986) A client-centered person/person-centered approach to therapy. In I Kutash and A Wolf (eds) Psychotherapist's Casebook. San Francisco: Jossey-Bass, pp. 197–208.

Chapter 16
The Counsellor as Prophet[1]

On becoming a prophet

This lecture seeks to honour the memory of a man who was always restless, who wanted to know more about everything, who lived life to the full and with passion. Not surprisingly, he was often difficult to live with for he tended to upset well-stocked apple-carts and to send shivers down the spines of those with vested interests whether in the medical, psychological or theological worlds. For those reasons I am encouraged to believe that Frank Lake[2] would have approved of a memorial lecture that is born of passionate intensity although I am only too aware, with WB Yeats, that passionate intensity is no guarantee against wrong-headedness or the worst kind of dogmatic arrogance. I acknowledge my fear that what I have to say this evening may well provoke hostility or, worse, that it may simply merit cynical indifference.

I am a reluctant prophet who feels temperamentally unsuited to the role. Prophets, as I conceptualise them from my reading of the Old Testament representatives of the species, are often angry, accusatory, courageous to the point of foolhardiness and, most significantly, men of God for whom the divine relationship leaves them with no option but to speak out. They are beacons, warning lights in periods of particular darkness when men and women (and particularly leaders) are in danger of losing their souls. They run the risk of being perceived as deluded visionaries, compulsive troublemakers, harbingers of doom – and they usually find themselves isolated and vulnerable. There are few who thank them for their efforts.

---

[1]This lecture was given as the Frank Lake Memorial Lecture on 14 July 1994. It was subsequently published by the Clinical Theology Association as Lingdale Paper 21 and is obtainable from the Association, St Mary's House, Church Westcote, Oxford, OX7 6SF.
[2]Dr Frank Lake, psychiatrist, evangelical Christian and the originator of Clinical Theology.

Such a role seems singularly inappropriate for someone who has spent all his working life in institutions. Prophets, I note, are usually outsiders, boundary people, somewhat eccentric figures whose calling makes them sit lightly to convention and renders them uncommonly impervious to the need for approval by the group or the community. And yet, as I reflect further, I realise with some anxiety that currently my own institutional allegiances have about them an air of provisionality. I come to suspect that I am sailing under flags of convenience which once suited my purposes but now seem increasingly incongruous. I am gradually drawn to the conclusion that I have been an outsider, a boundary person, all along but am now forced to acknowledge it and to accept the responsibilities that such a position imposes at times of crisis.

Some years ago I was invited to contribute to a book entitled *On Becoming a Psychotherapist* and I underwent the discipline of subjecting my life to rigorous scrutiny in order to elucidate why and how and when I had become a therapist. It was a task that, because of publishers' deadlines, I had to accomplish very rapidly and, looking back on it, I am faintly amazed by what was unearthed during that time of concentrated self-exploration. In the first place, I realised that almost from the moment of conception I had known the proximity of death. My mother suffered from a heart condition and giving birth to me almost resulted in her own death. I was her only child and when I entered the world I was a sickly, jaundiced and premature creature whose survival was by no means certain. Secondly, I came to see how deeply significant it was that I grew up during the Second World War. I was two and a half when war broke out with Nazi Germany and my childhood was spent with the whine of air-raid sirens constantly in my ears and with the nightly possibility of being exterminated by one of Hitler's bombs. Thirdly, I remembered the agony and the ecstasy of being naturally empathic. There was no choice in the matter, as I recall it. It was simply the case that I sensed what was going on in other people's minds and hearts and had to live with that knowledge. I still have a vivid memory of a teacher in my infants school who was mercilessly tormented by a class of over 60 children and whose suffering I shared imaginatively without having any power to alleviate it. She put her head in a gas oven one Saturday morning and I have never forgotten her.

These early experiences clearly affected me profoundly and as I reflect upon them I realise that they marked me at the outset as a boundary person. I became accustomed to moving between worlds, to traversing continually the gap between my own inner reality and that of others. Most importantly, perhaps, I learned what it meant to be alone and yet not alone.

As an only child who was constantly invited into the homes of others I knew the paradox of belonging and yet not belonging. Above all, however, there came the familiarity with the no man's land between life and death – the recognition of the permeability and fragility of existence. When I was 11 my grandfather and my uncle (his son) both died within three weeks of each other and, although I was grief-stricken, I was somehow prepared for the experience and saw it as part of the natural order of things. This, I am sure, was not unconnected to a mystical experience which I had on Good Friday 1946 when I was unexpectedly plunged into a deep apprehension of the Passion and Crucifixion of Christ and was overwhelmed by uncontrollable grief, which eventually gave way to a sense of peace and serenity. In short, before my childhood was over, I knew that life and death are not in opposition but belong to a greater unity and that to stand at the boundary between them is to be open to the world of spirit.

On being a therapist

In a sense I have never left this particular boundary country throughout my 26 years as a therapist. It seems to me that at any moment of the day or night a therapist might find himself or herself wrestling with the other's fear of death or, more devastatingly perhaps, with the allurement of death. Clients so often come to therapists because they are no longer sure that they can face life or that they can cope with death. They experience the utter loneliness of the boundary position and do not know where to turn. The therapist who is familiar with the terrain and who is safe in the knowledge of his or her own nature can be a loyal companion to the client who is stranded between life and death, but this boundary is no place for the faint-hearted: it demands courage that even the most conscientious companion cannot simulate. I am glad that I grew up in a world where it was commonplace to find courage on that boundary although I remain infinitely sad that a war was apparently needed to bring that about. There must be better ways of equipping us as a species to cope with our mortality and our immortality.

As I think on this matter I am all but overwhelmed by the wave of anger that floods through my being for I am caught up in the anguish of those clients in the past few years who have wrestled with the allurement of death because they could no longer see a place for themselves in the world. Many of them are young people in our universities and schools – intelligent, gifted, accomplished – and they are full of self-doubt and a prey to self-rejection. They have been taught that life means endless toil and competition, the pursuit of ever-greater achievement, the race for material affluence. And as a result they are in the grips of the icy fear of failure, they fantasise a life in the gutter, disowned, thrown out by a society characterised by built-in obsolescence and disposable commodities. Resounding in their ears are the slogans of cost effectiveness, performance-related pay, mission statements, total quality control and the brusque injunction of hard-nosed management: 'If it's too hot in the kitchen, get out.' When the whole of life has the feel of an over-heated kitchen, this cruel advice points ominously in one direction.

Other clients are not so young. For them the scrap heap is not a future fantasy but a present reality. They have been made redundant and have seen their life's work devalued or their role abolished. With the loss of work there has come a loss of self-respect and a deep sense of rejection leading often to depression and hopelessness. Others, again have been forced into premature retirement either because of massive restructuring policies or by ill-health brought on by the intolerable stress of ungovernable change. And then there are those who are still in employment but feel increasingly trapped in a vicious circle of overwork, unrealistic expectations and the permanent fear of adverse judgement. Donald Nicholl in an article in the Catholic journal *The Tablet* some months ago, coined a term that has stayed with me. He spoke of a 'culture of contempt' that he saw as permeating every area of our national life and finding its expression in the mindless and heartless implementation of policies directed at achieving greater efficiency at lower cost. This abject submission to the power of so-called market forces has created an atmosphere that breeds fear, ruthlessness and guilt. More recently the emphasis on competition and competitiveness has sought to disguise this prevailing ethos of neurosis and to cloak it as an admirable and necessary climate for personal satisfaction and national affluence. It is perhaps worthy of note that many of the most recent trumpetings on the obligatory virtue of competitiveness emanate from a man who amassed a personal fortune through his entrepreneurial aptitude, has been christened Tarzan by his admirers and was given the gift of a heart attack in Venice, which he has apparently squandered by not relinquishing his responsibilities.[3] A significant aspect for me, incidentally, of the tragedy of John Smith's[4] death was the fact that his heart gave up. It was as if the forces ranged against him were too great, the injustices too grotesque, the pain too enormous. I see him as a symbolic victim of a society that is wildly out of control because it has lost its heart.

Unique clients in a hostile world

As counsellor/prophet I want to give an unambiguous message. I know that in my consulting room whatever usefulness I have depends on my ability to convey to my client that he or she has unique value because he or she is. My success in communicating this existential validation of the personhood of the individual seeking my help will in turn depend on my genuine acceptance and on my willingness and capacity to understand his or her experiences. In brief, counselling brings healing because it

[3]Michael Heseltine, Conservative MP and former Deputy Prime Minister.
[4]Former Leader of the Labour Party.

offers affirmation of being, freedom from judgement and the strengthening that comes from being understood. This is the healing climate which experience tells me brings life and yet all around me I see the reverse – a climate which must inevitably be death-dealing because it is depersonalising, condemnatory and deaf to emotional pain. I see the effects of a political and economic philosophy that drives men and women to ever more desperate strategies to ensure their own continuing existence. Market forces engender impotence and divisiveness while rampant privatisation encourages a false belief in self-sufficiency that serves as a spurious armour to cope with the terror of being involved in a battle to the death for the survival of the fittest. I want to say loudly and clearly that my work and experience as a counsellor tell me that as a society we are doomed unless we can halt this catastrophic process in which we are all involved. If we don't we shall end up killing each other or surrendering what is left of our humanity to a dictator who will determine who should be exterminated or locked up.

Reflections on sexuality

Another of my early memories concerns women – or, more accurately, little girls. At junior school I had a devoted following. In some ways it was rather embarrassing, in others utterly delightful because it consisted entirely of girls. I can remember them now: Marilyn, Sylvia, Mary, Jennifer, Judith and Catherine. They would walk home with me and see me to the back garden gate. I don't remember much of what we talked about but I do recall the sense of being cherished and liked. With the passage of time the following diminished and by the age of nine or ten I was spending all my time with the boys and was totally caught up in cricket and football. For the next 15 years I lived in an almost completely male environment – public school, army, ancient university and then back to public school as a teacher of languages. For some time I wondered about my sexuality and was much attracted to writers of homosexual orientation. Looking back on it all, I believe now that I experienced what it meant to live on the boundary of the male and the female within my own personality. The study of language and literature greatly aided this particular boundary living for such study demands a willingness to enter into the most profound areas of human experience and to savour language at its most richly expressive – that is to say, language that attempts to do full justice to the whole range of male and female sensitivity and vulnerability. As a therapist I continue to live at this boundary and it is not without its risks. Many men regard male counsellors, for example, with great suspicion. They see them either as doing women's work or as seducers who wish to ensnare women in forced intimacy. Some women, too, avoid male therapists like the plague because they cannot believe in their trustworthiness. And yet to flee from this boundary area is to close oneself to that complexity of feeling, reason, intuition and sensation that so often constitutes the confusing terrain where clients risk losing themselves but also have the opportunity of discovering the nature of their own unique identities. I have come to love the male and the female in myself and increasingly value the boundary territory where the two converse with each other with serenity. Such converse remains vital, I know, if I am to continue to respond particularly to those many women in our society whom our culture threatens to condemn to half a life, to half an identity, to an existence so threaded through with the pernicious strands of patriarchy that there is little chance of fulfilment or of the realisation of the self. Living at the boundary of maleness and femaleness becomes a responsibility for any therapist who sees himself or herself as providing a sanctuary from the ravages of a culture and a society which clings to stereotypes as if they were bulwarks against disintegration.

What a hideous mess we seem to be in with our sexuality. It is perhaps scarcely surprising that of late it is over issues of sexuality that there appears to have been an orchestrated attack on the therapy professions by the mass media. Therapists have been seen in the pages of the *Guardian* as well as the *Telegraph* as seducers and abusers or as manipulators of the false memory syndrome. I am not suggesting that all therapists are innocent of sexual malpractice but the consistency and the vehemence of many of the recent attacks would indicate a far deeper malaise. In the face of widespread marital breakdown, of child abuse by both men and women on a massive scale, of public figures who betray their partners or indulge in self-destructive sexual practices, of a resurgence of prejudice against the gay community, of the frightening reticence about AIDS – in the face of all this the popular press, it seems, is driven to attack one of the few professions which day in, day out comes alongside the pain, the fear and the despair resulting from sexual and physical alienation and confusion. The therapists are the witnesses of society's radical sexual disorder and in the same way that a murderer must be rid of witnesses to his crime so society must make a scapegoat of the therapists so that the appalling sickness is pushed back into the shadows. Ultimately, however, the strategy must fail for the sexual woundedness within our culture is too deep and too widespread to be concealed. The same self-denigration that is encouraged by the economic and political policies of our day is intensified by the prejudice, secrecy and hypocrisy that surround our sexual lives. So often the humiliation experienced in other areas of life leads to the abuse of power in the sexual sphere as intolerable pain seeks alleviation in sexual excess. What is more, the cultivated unawareness of materialistic men and women can result in a complete denial of sexual exploitation and brutality where it so evidently exists. Physical denigration is closely allied to sexual confusion and it is not irrelevant that eating disorders have become increasingly prevalent in recent years often prompted by the demands of an image-conscious society or by the stress engendered by a profound sense of powerlessness. We vilify our bodies because we cannot bear the sense of our own unacceptability and inadequacy. It is as if in desperation we seek to endow ourselves with beauty and power but only succeed in making ourselves as grotesque and helpless as the inmates of a concentration camp. Faced by the feverish face of a skeletal figure in a voluminous jumper who should have been a beautiful young woman made for personal and sexual fulfilment, how can a counsellor do other than inwardly weep and rage?

As counsellor/prophet, I am forced to utter a solemn warning. As a species we are in danger of bringing about our own sterility and destruction because we are refusing to embrace, honour and cherish the bodies that we are and to affirm and harness the source of our creativity which is our sexuality. We need to unleash a torrent of tenderness upon ourselves and each other so that we can celebrate our wholeness including our genitals and cease to be frightened of ourselves and of each other. If this sounds Utopian and absurd then I would claim that in our heart of hearts we know that nothing less will do if we are to turn back the raging flood of sexual aberration and despair which currently threatens to engulf us.

What of the Church?

I spoke earlier of sailing under flags of convenience as far as my institutional allegiances are concerned and there are many occasions when I wonder if this has been the case with my membership of the Church. I can recall nostalgically the time when faith seemed relatively uncomplicated and when I could experience the warmth and security of the liturgy and the gentle embrace of the church community. I have been jolted out of this comfortable ambience by a number of factors that are in many ways a direct outcome of my work as a therapist. It has been a source of pain for me over many years to encounter, either as clients or as acquaintances, many people who have suffered unspeakably at the hands of organised religion. They have been made to feel wicked, guilty and, most terrifying of all, utterly unlovable. Such feelings have often been engendered by the imposition of judgemental and dogmatic beliefs in the name of a loving God who laid down his life that others might live. The damage wrought on individuals by such practices is often incalculable especially when the people involved are already vulnerable and have been much undermined by life's experiences. Sadly the perpetrators of such psychological violence – and representatives of other faiths and philosophies as well as Christianity must be included – rarely recognise the devastation caused by their behaviour and attitudes, but as a counsellor I am only too familiar with the often long-standing pain of those who have suffered at their hands. It is this repeated experience of accompanying the casualties of punitive religion that has forced me to re-assess the interpretation of much Christian doctrine and the impact of certain traditional practices. In some ways this has been a rewarding experience for not infrequently I have discovered beneath the powerful dominance of fall and redemption theology, with its emphasis on original sin, human wickedness and the need for self-negation, another stream of belief that affirms the unremitting and unconditional love of God for humanity and the whole of creation and the potential divinisation of humankind. The God whom I meet in this tradition is the infinitely compassionate mother and father and lover of Julian of Norwich's revelations, the joyful, paradoxical, almost teasing, God of Meister Eckhart, the source and goal of Teilhard de Chardin's evolutionary order, the life-giving, infinitely nurturing God of Matthew Fox's creation theology. This is a neglected orthodoxy that lies below the surface of so much that passes for the Christian message and that turns on its head the guilt-inducing worm theology that engenders a fear of God's condemnation and rejection rather than an awareness of his unshakeable and unchanging love for the noblest beings of his creation, which we are.

Neglected orthodoxy as it might be, however, I have discovered that to hold to such ideas is to be regarded by some as a threat and a danger within the Church community. And yet my experience both in my own life and in the sharing of the struggles which many of my clients endure leaves me with no option. There is something about being a therapist – at least in the tradition that I have chosen – which in the end leaves no possible escape from honesty and no remaining bolt-hole for the sophisticated practice of self-deception. In some ways this is a sure recipe for metaphorical martyrdom because most of us most of the time are not over-keen to look too closely at our underlying assumptions, especially when these are an integral part of a belief structure or value system that has informed our living for some time. It is for this reason that both churches and schools of therapy, too, find it hard to tolerate those individuals who dare to trust their own experience and judgement and as a result cast doubt upon the received wisdom whether of a theological or psychological nature. For the individual himself or herself the struggle to be honest – or, to use the jargon of person-centred therapy, the resolve to be congruent – is fraught with danger. Not only is there the well-nigh certainty of adverse judgement from others but, more devastating still, there is the inevitable agony of self-doubt, the fear of *folie de grandeur,* the self-accusation of arrogance. At times I have felt the full force of these internal conflicts, often inflamed by hostile external forces, and the temptation to recant, to step back into line whether theologically or psychologically has been irresistible. I simply could not bear the pain and readily excused my cowardice on the grounds that masochism is a neurosis or, better still, that humility is a virtue.

Interestingly enough, the theological struggle has become easier in recent times. Since the publication of my little book *Behold the Man* in 1991 I have had the immense consolation of receiving many letters and not a few invitations from those who are also clearly struggling in boundary territory. For me it has been particularly revealing to discover that many such people are members of religious orders. They have already committed their lives to God and often to a way of contemplation and yet it is precisely they who find themselves at odds with much that has characterised church attitudes and practice in the past. In some of my most despairing moments, when I have felt myself to be on the very edge of the 'household of faith', I have drawn the greatest comfort from the shared perceptions of contemplative monks and nuns who have written, sometimes from a distance of many thousand of miles, because they have found in the pages of *Behold the Man* a fellow pilgrim in the boundary country.

As counsellor/prophet, I have passionate words to say to my fellow Christians and to the Christian churches. I believe that our hour is coming and that we shall fail to grasp it unless we are prepared to accept the responsibility of having God within us. I tremble as I utter those words and I sense that in doing so I am experiencing the prophet's greatest burden: this is the point where I am open to the most violent attacks from without and from within. I have to withstand the voice that tells me that masochism is a neurosis and humility a virtue. If I truly believe that God is within me then it goes without saying that God is in everyone however obscured or denied. It is this truth that the churches must now urgently proclaim but (and here come the really difficult bit) in order to do so they have to launch a full-scale onslaught on spiritual blindness in high places. In doing this, I maintain, they will be keeping very close to the example of their Founder who died because he challenged the leaders of his day for their hypocrisy, blindness and hardness of heart. As Christians we must resolutely oppose everyone and everything that threatens to devalue persons, to condemn rather than to redeem, to inflict pain rather than bring healing, to take away rather than to give, to deceive rather than to illuminate. Most importantly we must oppose those tendencies within ourselves that make us wilfully blind and prone to put expediency before people, personal cost before the relief of suffering, love of power before justice. I can scarcely bear the embarrassment of uttering these words for I feel a prig, the most inflated kind of preacher, a holy Joe. And yet why should I not say these things for, after all, I have tried to keep close to my God for most of my life? What is more I know what it feels like to fall flat on my face like the servant in Julian of Norwich's wonderful vision and to discover that God has not ceased to watch over me in my desolation. And I have tried to be true to my calling as a counsellor, which means that I have committed my life not to poverty, chastity and obedience but to acceptance, empathy and congruence. I have in this sense been living under discipline for 26 years and during that time I calculate that I have had the privilege of accompanying more than 3,000 souls on some part of their journey home to themselves and to God. I speak, therefore, with authority.

Sharing the journey

For me, every new counselling relationship marks the beginning of an unpredictable adventure. There can be no certainty about where I am to travel with my client or of the nature of the companionship that he or she will require. Mercifully most clients are modest enough in their needs. They want a compassionate, listening and understanding ear, warmth without sentimentality, willingness on the part of the counsellor not to simulate, a preparedness to be faithful in the accompaniment and not to abandon. But every so often – and for me in recent years it has become disconcertingly often – there comes the person whose journey, if it is to be embarked upon, requires a companion who is more intrepid and willing to venture into the unknown where there are few reassuring reference points and no clear destination. The suicidal, the abused, those who have never bonded, those aggressed in the womb are but a few of the persons who have challenged me to go with them to the extreme limit of the relationship boundary. As so often in this extraordinary profession, I wish it were otherwise. I don't want to be *that* significant for another person for I know that I cannot finally give meaning to another's existence. I don't want the burden of carrying hope: I don't want the task of relating at this depth; I don't want to be loved – and hated – so blindly or so passionately; I cannot bear the sense of combined responsibility and powerlessness. Inside, I am protesting: 'I am not God. I am not ultimate reality. I cannot love you into life.'

What does all that mean when we get down to brass tacks? For me it has meant going to the very edge of trust in some of my therapeutic relationships. It has involved facing the implications of believing that we have it within us to become the people we are uniquely equipped to be if only we can offer each other the conditions for such becoming. Such trusting, difficult at any time, is increasingly hazardous in the present climate of our society. Violence is all around us; the abuse of human-beings both of themselves and of each other has reached epidemic proportions; government policies encourage us to trust no one, to be in permanent competition, to evaluate, appraise and assess everyone and everything, to assume incompetence and corruption everywhere. The core conditions of the person-centred approach to counselling have seldom seemed so naive, so counter-cultural, so open to derision and contempt. It is in such a climate that I am challenged to trust my own integrity and that of my client, to believe in the universal yearning for wholeness, to risk failure, to run the danger of being seen as the fool who drowned in the deep waters of intimacy because he was mad enough to trust that he and his companion would somehow reach dry land.

What of counsellors?

Once more I am feeling uncomfortable, this time not because of my fear of inflation but because I have an anxiety that for many of my fellow counsellors – from within the person-centred tradition as well as from other orientations – what I have just said will sound like pretentious nonsense or a kind of mystical hysteria. I have a glimpse of po-faced figures sitting around large tables in prestigious places, debating ethics and standards, deliberating on criteria for accreditation, reporting on the government's stance on vocational qualifications. Or again, I am imprisoned in a nightmarish library of ever proliferating books on counselling and therapy each advocating – often in cheerless and leaden prose – the efficacy of its particular brand or reviling with varying degrees of venom the offerings of a rival school. Another nightmare features two armies – the counsellors and the psychotherapists – fighting bitterly over the same terrain and each proclaiming their incontrovertible right to occupation. Again, I can speak with authority for I have sat at those large tables, I have contributed to that Quatermass-type body of literature, I have been wounded on the battlefield between counsellors and psychotherapists.

As counsellor/prophet I feel some of the greatest despair as I turn to address those from my own world of professional therapy. Is this the place, I wonder, where I can expect to have the least honour and to command the least respect? I fear so and yet I have no option but to go on. I believe that we therapists have an opportunity, like the churches, to affect the course of human history if we can but seize the moment. We are the guardians of knowledge given us by countless suffering individuals who seek our help. That knowledge is deeply personal and because of that very fact, as Carl Rogers pointed out long ago, it has about it a profound and contemporary universality. It is not fanciful, I believe, to see the counsellors and therapists of our day as the chief recipients of the collective pain and yearning of the age. This is a treasure beyond price but its value lies in its capacity, if fully revealed and articulated, to give meaning to present distress and to provide hope and guidance for the future. To my colleagues in the therapy profession I would urge the need to break silence, to speak with authority, to stay true to experience and to refuse to be shouted down. Sadly, though, we shall only have the courage to do this – and the possibility of being truly heard – if we are united.

It is a mark of the past decade that, one by one, the professions have been undermined in our country. The teachers, the doctors, the social

workers, the lawyers, the civil servants, the university lecturers – the list
is long of those bodies of people, mainly in the helping and service
professions, who have suffered vilification and whose confidence has
been seriously eroded and whose morale has been fatally enfeebled.
Most frequently the process is accelerated and reinforced by disunity in
the ranks of the profession itself as some seek to gauge where the power
lies and to play their cards in order to win advantage. All the signs are
there that this same process is permeating through the ranks of the
fledgling profession of therapy and counselling. Power-mongering is rife
even to the extent of falsifying the supposed edicts and intentions of
parliaments both in London and Strasbourg in order to engender fear in
rival parties. If this despicable behaviour persists we shall have no
chance of finding and maintaining the unity that I believe will be essential if we are to give powerful voice to the knowledge that we, and
perhaps we alone, possess.

Human and divine

Throughout much of his life Frank Lake wrestled to reconcile his psychological discoveries and understandings with his theological grasp of
reality. In this respect, as in many others, he was himself prophetic.
Increasingly, now, therapists whether Christian, humanist or of other
faiths, seek to integrate their psychological and spiritual experience.
Indeed, it is thanks to Lake and others like him that the spiritual is
regarded by increasing numbers of therapists as an essential component
in the understanding of human nature and in the conduct of therapy. For
me this process of integration is often perplexing and demanding but to
duck it is no longer possible. As a final tribute to Frank Lake I want to
end this lecture with my own current attempt to make sense of my life
and work as a Christian and as a counsellor. It is a kind of prophetic
utterance to myself and its implications lie in the mysterious future. It
may be that some of you will recognise at least a part of your own struggles in my attempt to articulate what must ultimately remain inexpressible.

I have come to believe that as a person-centred counsellor I am
involved in the practice of a discipline that has all the marks of a spiritual
vocation. What is more – and here comes the rub for some I suspect –
the nature of the spiritual path that is being pursued is quintessentially
Western, Christian and incarnational. It rests upon a belief in the transformation of uniquely differentiated persons through the experience
both of offering and being offered a relationship characterised by acceptance where there was rejection, understanding where there was indifference, mutuality where there was abuse of power. It is a spiritual path
that needs no liturgy beyond itself, no monastery for its perfecting. It
demands not self-negation but the self-forgetfulness which comes from
self-love engendered though relationship. Its deeply Christian roots are

perhaps most exemplified by its mirroring of the Trinitarian concept of God, the most inspired of all Christian doctrines that sees God himself or herself as a relationship. The person of God the Father, according to this doctrine, has no separate being apart from the person of the Son and the Spirit who continually dances between them: wholeness is possible only in and through relationship and the wholeness thus experienced is greater than the sum of the two persons in their separateness. That, to my mind, is the most profound description of the therapeutic relationship in the person-centred tradition and enables me to grasp why it is that there are moments in my work as a therapist when I feel outside time and space and cannot conceive that heaven itself could be more desirable. I have no inclination to analyse those moments but they are characterised for both my client and me by a sense of radical unconditional, unearned acceptance and by an empowerment that makes us capable, however briefly, of loving the whole created order. In short, we have ourselves been swept up into the divine relationship. To the doubtless irritation of many of my professional colleagues in the counselling world I cannot resist adding that Christianity long ago coined words to describe this experience: my client and I, to employ this strangely distant language, are justified by grace and permeated by sanctification. For a moment, however fleeting, we are whole and holy, fully human and therefore the incarnation of the divine. Accuse me of blasphemy if you dare.

References

Dryden W, Spurling L (eds) (1989) On Becoming a Psychotherapist. London: Tavistock/Routledge.
Nicholl D (1993) A culture of contempt. The Tablet (6 November): 1442–4.
Thorne BJ (1991) Behold the Man. London: Darton, Longman & Todd.

Part III
All Shall be Well

Introduction

I have lived in Norwich since 1973. This section of the book is in some ways a celebration of and a vote of thanks to a 'fine city'. Norwich is a remarkable place for many reasons but not least because of its religious inheritance. In the Middle Ages Norwich stood next to London in importance both as a commercial centre and as a place of learning and religious devotion. It was a city where the secular and the sacred intermingled; alongside the prosperous exporters and manufacturers there lived a host of monks and nuns in more than 20 different monasteries and convents, the biggest of them being the Benedictine priory with the old Norman cathedral at its heart. Above all, too, there were churches in abundance and even today there are 32 surviving medieval churches within the old city walls.

To walk the streets of Norwich is to be constantly reminded of this rich, spiritual history. What is more, for counsellors and psychotherapists there is the permeating influence of the remarkable anchoress, Julian of Norwich, who in the fourteenth century received a series of visions that she later set down in the first book to be written by a woman in English. *The Revelations of Divine Love* first fell into my hands in 1962 when I was setting out on my career as a school teacher. It contains astonishing insights into the nature of God, who is experienced by Julian as unconditionally loving and totally devoid of judgement. He does not even forgive because He has never accused in the first place. For me Julian is the perfect antidote to the kind of judgemental religion that still holds many twentieth century men and women in thrall. Her book never ceases to astonish me and to reveal new treasures. It is also profoundly reassuring to remember that Julian was a counsellor in Norwich 600 years ago when England was in turmoil and life bitter and cruel for most people. And yet Julian never gives up hope; her vision of God and her

103

deep belief in the essential belovedness of all humanity enables her to proclaim that 'all shall be well' despite the pain, the sin and the horror she sees around her.

For me it was a great privilege to be invited to give the annual 'Julian Lecture' in 1993 and this forms Chapter 17. In this lecture I attempt to show something of what I believe to have been Julian's skill as a counsellor. Person-centred practitioners will readily understand why I see her as a precursor of the approach and they will perhaps not be surprised to know that in the training of person-centred therapists at the University of East Anglia, Julian features on the timetable. A further justification for this inclusion of a medieval mystic in the training of twentieth-century therapists is offered in the foreword that I provided for John Michael Mountney's book *Sin Shall be a Glory*. I believe that what I wrote then about the pernicious influence of our competitive, accountability culture remains just as true today and has in no way been ameliorated by the recent change of government in our country.

Chapters 19 and 20 are published here for the first time. They are lectures given in an environment of serious fun at the Old Rectory in Great Melton near Norwich during a series of 'professional holidays' for therapists and members of the helping professions that took place in the mid-1980s. I include them because they recall for me how much easier it is to reflect on matters of the deepest concern when there is a spirit of gentle humour around. For me, too, they reflect another of the qualities for which Norwich has earned my endless gratitude. In a city with such a history there reigns a sense of balance, of perspective that somehow tempers despair. At the Old Rectory in Great Melton it was possible to relax, to draw breath and to discover that Time could be domesticated and that we could tap into eternity and glimpse the wonder of our own natures. In some ways it was rather like Finchden Manor, the remarkable 'house of hospitality' that George Lyward founded for disturbed adolescents in the 1930s and that I describe in Chapter 20. Such places are rare and our society stands desperately in need of them.

Chapter 17
Julian of Norwich: Radical Psychotherapist[1]

This is an age of change, fear and disintegration. If that sounds over the top, then you must forgive the skewed perspective of someone who, day in and day out, tries to respond to the pain of those who pour out their minds and hearts in the security of the counselling room. If the truth be told, however, counsellors and psychotherapists, as the twentieth century draws to a close, constitute a beleaguered profession and may perhaps be excused for believing that humankind has moved into a dark and perilous phase in its history. As waiting lists grow longer and the concerns and difficulties of clients apparently more complex and appalling, the therapist has no option but to stay true to his or her own experience and to confront the reality of the flood of psychic pain that threatens to engulf everything. Hope, if it is to be found, does not lie in dismissive rationalisations that find expression in such statements as 'it's not that bad' or 'every age has believed it is facing the ultimate crisis'. Even less is hope to be found in the naïve but still prevalent belief that science and technology will at the eleventh hour come up with the answers and deliver the world from the jaws of disaster. Authentic hope always lies through and beyond despair and is seldom discovered without moving into the darkness and risking the loss of the few remaining reference points that seem to make some sense of the bewildering landscape.

In recent times, it is as if the therapists' frightening knowledge has erupted onto the front pages of the daily newspapers. We read reports almost every day of the disintegration of what we had previously taken to be 'normal'. It is no longer possible to speak of a 'normal' family or a 'normal' marriage: interpersonal violence has reached the point where children are ritually tortured and 10-year olds kill infants. Addiction is

[1]This lecture was delivered as the annual 'Julian Lecture' at St Julian's Church, Norwich on 8 May 1993. It was subsequently published in 1995, in part, in the *Fairacres Chronicle*, 28(1): 17–26 and is reprinted with permission of the publishers, SLG Press.

rife and drugs, whether prescribed or illicit, shield millions from the reality of pain and plunge them into even more unimaginable nightmares.

It is not only in our relationships, however, that violence has finally reduced the concept of normality to meaninglessness. It is no longer possible, for example, to speak of a 'normal' career. Anyone who has experienced the pain of unemployment or redundancy will know something of the violence, internal and external, which surrounds the 'execution' of a person's aspirations or of his or her self-concept. The assaults upon personal identity in a volatile employment situation are legion and our country is now littered with those whose humiliation and depression are but the outward garments of rage and a sense of seething injustice. What is more, for many millions who remain in employment or in the education system there is now the pervasive and insidious poison of the competitive, accountability culture. There are those who thrive on it, of course. Efficiency, appraisal, financial accountability make a fine trinity on which to hang many a high-sounding moral principle. But it is often an evil trinity for it can create unprecedented stress and anxiety and a climate of distrust where big brother is not only sitting in the next office but comes to reside in the inner sanctuary of a person's own mind. The suicide of the managing director is as likely as the depression of the laid-off labourer. Behind the current battle over testing in our schools and aside from the very real issues of excessive work demands on teachers, there resides, I suspect, a profoundly more significant and symbolic struggle. Raising standards, improving the quality of teaching, providing evidence of achievement – they all sound worthy objectives and they appeal to those who relish hitting targets and obtaining hard data. But many teachers know – even those who find it difficult to express themselves with adequate feeling – that learning depends ultimately on love, love between teachers and taught, and love for the subjects that are being studied. Testing is about judgement and where that judgement is divorced from the relationship between teacher and pupil, then the spirit of learning easily withers and trust ebbs away. What is more when testing becomes the principal cornerstone of the educational edifice then the building loses warmth and becomes inhospitable and eventually uninhabitable. The battle over testing is about loss of love, loss of tenderness, loss of imagination, loss of trust, loss of soul. And the sad thing is that these words of mine will make no sense to those who believe that they are right and that I am a woolly-minded liberal whose gravest misfortune was to have been educated in the 1950s and brainwashed in the 1960s.

The mounting pain among clients who seek therapeutic help is perhaps unimaginable for those whose lives remain comparatively untouched by the swirling eddies of change – although I sense that such people are now members of a dwindling minority. It is not easy to convey the agony of it all without sounding hysterical or histrionic and yet there are days when I return home haunted by the vision of our culture as a great open wound. Never, it seems, has the search for intimacy been so desperate and yet all around relationships are in turmoil, violence is erupting in the home and on the streets and, as global economic and ecological disaster seems increasingly possible, competitive materialism is revealed for the treacherous cul-de-sac that it is.

Many people who cross the therapist's threshold are caught up in the paralysing fear of adverse judgement. Their level of stress and anxiety is so great that they have lost all confidence in their own ability to function effectively or to make decisions. They go in fear of ridicule, condemnation and of rejection whether from the workplace or the family circle. The broken marriage, the redundancy notice, the escalating anxiety are but the outward signs of an inner desolation where there is no let-up from the ever-present feelings of failure and worthlessness. There are others who bring with them the unspeakable burden of self-hate. It is as if they defend themselves from the adverse judgement of others by passing the ultimate judgement on themselves in order, somehow, to deaden the pain and to anaesthetise themselves against intolerable anxiety. For the counsellor, there can scarcely be a more demanding task than that of accompanying a person who is clearly sensitive, intelligent and beautiful but whose self-hate is so virulent that he or she experiences only total unacceptability. Such persons often subject their bodies to the most vile abuse in a desperate attempt to exert some power over lives that are grotesquely out of control or to experience momentary relief from the total numbness that self-hate frequently engenders. The rise in eating disorders in our society, for example, is alarming and in almost all cases there is a large element of self-hate or self-disgust in the sufferer.

In recent years therapists have had to bear the opening of another Pandora's box. With sickening regularity now men and women of all ages bring their stories of sexual and physical abuse, usually within their own families or intimate circles. These accounts come from people of all sections of society and sadly from many who are of the 'household of faith'. The abuse has sometimes gone on for many years and points to a disordering of sexuality and physicality that seems to be of epidemic proportions. Those who have suffered in this way usually hold themselves as in some way responsible and therefore drag out their lives beneath a formidable load of inappropriate guilt. Those who perpetrate the abuse, on the other hand, are often unable to accept the implications of what they have done and seek to defend themselves or even block off from any memory of what has occurred. For me in recent times it has come as cold comfort to discover that women are as capable of abuse as men and that for many persons the lovely word 'mother' is as defiled as the word 'father' is for others. The sea of pain around the issues of abuse is vast and there are days when I dread going to my counsellor's office in case I have to listen to yet another story of unimaginable horror. Each time it happens I have to face the fact that so many in our human family do not know how to treasure their bodies and their sexuality and that what should be primary channels for loving have become instruments for torture, humiliation and terror.

The fear of adverse judgement, the burden of self-hate, the agony of abuse contribute mightily to the enormous pools of pain in which increasingly, it seems, so many people must contend in almost every sphere of their lives. For them there can be no trust in relationships and no safety in the universe. The yearning to love and to be loved is stifled to be replaced instead by a constant watchfulness and defensiveness against hostile invaders. Not surprisingly, a sense of futility and meaning-lessness is never far away and this is intensified by loneliness and alien-ation from family, community and any form of rootedness. Lonely people, belonging nowhere and to nobody, are left to cope as best they can in a world that has declared itself to be implacably indifferent. When asked, 'What is the most important question a person can ask?', Albert Einstein is said to have replied, 'Is the universe a friendly place or not?' For most clients who come to the counsellor and psychotherapist there can be only one answer to that searching question and it is a resounding 'no'. In a sinister and collusive way, too, in recent years the human immunodeficiency virus has reinforced on the biological plane the desperation that for many is only too manifest on the psychological plane. In the face of such a hostile environment what response can there logically be except one of cynicism and hopelessness? The therapist's task is thus formidable for he or she has somehow to rekindle hope in the client's heart and that is impossible without the rediscovery of trust. It is as if the therapist must become the representative of a different order and through his or her own response to the client convey that, despite all the seeming evidence to the contrary, there is the possibility of a positive force at the centre of life that is more fundamental than the direst destructiveness. It is the living out of that hope which becomes the therapist's most urgent responsibility and what therefore matters above everything else is his or her belief about human nature, the created order and the meaning of life. Psychological skills, therapeutic insights, sophisticated medication may all have their part to play in the process of healing but, as St Paul put it in another context, without love they are likely in the end to profit nothing. That is a hard lesson for any therapist and not one that greatly enhances a sense of professional identity. It demands a commitment to penetrate behind the surface of things and to risk discovering whether or not there is any substance to life as we know it. It goes to the heart of the matter; in short, it is the challenge of radical psychotherapy.

When Dame Margery Kempe visited Mother Julian of Norwich about 1415 the latter was 72 years old. Her reputation as a counsellor seems to have spread widely by this time for it is clear that Margery was not the only one to visit her on pilgrimage. In many ways it is remarkable that Julian had survived for so long. She had lived through three outbreaks of the Black Death, she had seen England ravaged by disease, food shortage and bankruptcy brought about by the relentless Hundred Years War with France. She had witnessed the collapse of law and order on many occasions and the cruel suppression by her own Bishop of the peasants' uprising in 1380. She had also seen the rise of the lay reform movement in the Church led by John Wyclif and the subsequent persecution of the Lollards after the horrendous statute De Heretico Comburendo in 1401. In short, she had lived through a period of tumultuous change and suffering and one that must have thrown most of her contemporaries into a state of utter cynicism and despair. What is more, it is a period characterised by the incessant battle for power whether for property and rights or for men's minds. The old order is collapsing and there is chaos and fear as a new order struggles to be born. It is not difficult to imagine that for most people it was an age of anguish, unpredictability and the constant fear of death, whether through illness or the aggression of others.

Margery Kempe goes to Julian because she, too, at this time is the subject of adverse and punitive judgement and is ravaged by guilt. She is a passionate woman and her very intensity has led her into trouble. She is so overwhelmed with feeling at times of public worship that she continually bursts into tears and as a result causes much disquiet to others. She is mortified by her behaviour but seems powerless to stop it; even in the street she is liable to burst into tears when thinking of Christ's Passion. Understandably, perhaps, many people became exasperated with Margery and told her in no uncertain terms to restrain her weeping. Ecclesiastical and social sanctions were used against her and she was even thrown out of church in her own home town of Lynn and forbidden to speak. There were others who suggested she should wear a different style of clothing! In short, when Margery arrived in Norwich to consult Julian we may imagine that she had lost confidence in the meaning of her experience and was feeling condemned and rejected by her contemporaries and by the church authorities. We may conjecture that she was close to condemning her own nature and full of doubt about its trustworthiness.

Julian's reception of Margery provides us with a precious and unique insight into her work as a counsellor. What is more, it is the client's record that we possess for Julian never herself wrote of her encounters with those in trouble; she knew, it would seem, all about the code of confidentiality! It is clear that Julian did not rush in to give advice. Margery tells us that they held 'holy conversation' for an extended time and that she was able to tell Julian in detail about her revelations and experiences and 'of the very many holy speeches and conversations' that she had had with Jesus. Julian, it seems, received Margery with friendship and trust. She listens and enters into Margery's experience with respect and increasing thankfulness. She is concerned not to judge but to make it safe for Margery to express herself fully in all her confusion and ecstasy. When she finally speaks it is to validate Margery's experience and to counsel obedience to the will of God as revealed in the depth of her own soul. Margery quotes Julian's words: 'The Holy Spirit never moves anything against love, for if he did, he would be contrary to his own self – for he is all Love.' Of the tiresome tears, Julian speaks with tenderness and with the utmost conviction. The tears, she says, are the greatest proof Margery could wish for that the Holy Spirit does indeed dwell in her soul. No evil spirit can give such signs, she says, and quotes both St Paul and St Jerome in support of her understanding. St Jerome, according to Julian, says that 'tears torment the devil more than do the pains of hell'.

We can imagine the immense relief that must have flooded through Margery as she talked with Julian. Here was someone who was prepared to trust her, to be her soulmate rather than her judge or accuser. Here was someone, too, who would listen in detail and in depth and who, having done so, could restore her faith in the wholesomeness of her own nature and the trustworthiness of her experience. Margery quotes Julian again: 'Holy Writ says the soul of a righteous man is the dwelling-place of God; and so I trust, dear sister, that you are.' Not that Julian in any way underrates the battle that Margery will continue to experience in the face of her opponents and those who deride her nature and her experiences. 'Set all your trust in God,' she says, 'and do not fear the language of the world, for the more despising, shame and reproof that you have in the world, the more is your merit in the sight of God. Patience is necessary for you, for in that you shall keep your soul.' Margery goes on her way greatly cheered. Her confidence is restored in God, in herself, in the legitimacy of her feelings, in the rightness of speaking out. Julian's response to her is of friend to friend and she shows infinite tenderness and compassion as befits the exchange between two lovers of Christ. At the same time, Julian in no way evades the truth that for the passionate and impulsive Margery life will continue to be tough. 'Patience is necessary for you' she says and at these words we may be sure that Margery nodded in instant agreement. She knew that she was known. (Butler-Bowden, 1936)

In the encounter with Margery Kempe we discover a Julian who displays the kind of capacity to respond to a human-being in distress which is the fruit of a life spent in communion with the God who dwells in the depths of her own soul. Julian, the counsellor, embodies the authority of one who has dared to be intimate with God and who can no longer keep to herself the knowledge which flows from that intimacy. It is striking that Margery does not refer to the 'Showings', which are, of course, the consummate outpouring of Julian's own love affair with God and it is clear that Julian herself does not mention her book to Margery although the conclusion of the long text was being written as long ago as 1393. Margery's apparent ignorance of the existence of Julian's writings is the more surprising because she rather prided herself on being up with all the latest theological and devotional treatises. I am inclined to believe that the most likely reason for Margery's unawareness is the comparative hiddenness of Julian's book. Indeed, scholars have been baffled why there are singularly few surviving copies of Julian's work in contrast to the veritable plethora of extant copies of the writings of such people as Richard Rolle, Walter Hilton and the author of *The Cloud of Unknowing*. Could it be that the reason lies in the book's revolutionary and radical insights? Julian was clearly a person of high intelligence and no little sophistication despite her claims to be 'unlettered'. What is more she must have known that her book in the wrong hands could lead to all kinds of trouble. She was, I suspect, far too wise to make herself a sitting target for the secular or the ecclesiastical authorities. She had no desire, I suspect, to be an unnecessary martyr. She had, after all, at the age of 30 already risked death (and accepted it) in order to be taken up into the love of her Lord and her task was to communicate what she had learned. It is not, I believe, fanciful to suggest that while it was imperative for her to write her book, it was equally important for the book to be kept under wraps and restricted to a limited circulation until the time came when it was safe to assume that it would not be destroyed by those who had every reason to fear its message. It seems that it was to be two-and-a-half centuries before that time came and that it is only in our own era that the full significance of her experiences is gradually emerging. Even now, I believe, Julian's 'Revelations' are so utterly amazing in their implications that there are few who, in Blake's words, can 'bear such beams of love'. And yet in my work as a therapist I come with awe and trembling to the belief that the radical psychotherapy that so many in our generation cry out for demands a preparedness on the part of those in my profession to risk being blinded by the dazzling light shining from every page of a book that a devout seventeenth-century scribe-editor, fearful that it should fall into the wrong hands, described as 'the sublime and wonderful revelations of the unutterable love of God, in Jesus Christ vouchsafed to a dear lover of his, and in her to all his dear friends and lovers whose hearts like hers do flame in the love of our dearest Jesus.'

Julian's writing is often so measured and carefully worked over that the unsuspecting reader may fail to see at first that her book is a passionate love story. What is more, beginning as it does with a focus on the suffering of Jesus during his Passion, the modern reader may initially be repelled by the apparent dwelling on the physical gruesomeness of torture and crucifixion. Nor does Julian spare her reader the details of her own near-death experience during which she received her revelations. It is only gradually that we begin to understand that the body is central to Julian's understanding of God and of herself. Her book is addressed to embodied souls and not to disembodied spirits. The Jesus whom she beholds and loves is a man of flesh who bleeds and thirsts and embraces. The human body for her is something of supreme beauty so that she can speak even of the act of excretion with awe and wonder. The tactile quality of Julian's imagery is sometimes breathtaking. She speaks of God's relationship to us, for example, in words which belong to the bridal chamber: 'And in the joining and the union he is our very true spouse and we his beloved wife and his fair maiden, with which wife he was never displeased, for he says: I love you and you love me, and our love will never divide in two' (58th chapter) (Colledge and Walsh, 1978, p. 293).

The body, however, is only the beginning of Julian's hymn of praise and delight as she celebrates the discoveries she had made about human nature. Gradually the reader begins to experience the passion that flows through Julian's pen. How Julian loves what she calls her 'even Christians'! It is for love that she must communicate what she has learned for she sees how miserable and desperate so many of her fellow human beings are. Time and again she assures us that it is only natural and inevitable that we should sometimes feel depressed and empty and that life is by definition a series of ups and downs. The truth, however, is that God regards us as the noblest thing he has ever made, that we are his 'darlings' and that he never ceases to love us no matter what we feel and no matter what we do. If we could but see ourselves with the eyes of God, Julian suggests, we should know assuredly that we are wondrous creatures and that we have within us all the properties of the God who made us, all the properties that is of the mother and the father and the lover that God is.

This is astonishing stuff but Julian insists on it time and time again. This is why she wrestles so fiercely with the problem of sin. How can these wondrous creatures that we are perpetrate such vile deeds? In the end Julian must accept a mystery but not before she has concluded that sin is, in some important way, necessary and that our very sins can become medals of honour. God, she sees, does not cease to love us when we sin; indeed we do not even fall in his eyes because he knows that in the deepest recesses of our being (what she calls out substance) we have no desire to sin at all. Nothing is more painful to God – and more wasteful – than a person's self-recrimination. God does not even have to forgive us because he has not accused us in the first place. If we sin, we have through our shame and sadness, a wonderful opportunity to be utterly vulnerable, completely childlike and in this state to run to our mother God to find there immediate acceptance, a continuing confirmation of our identity as her beloved, her darling whom she will never abandon.

Julian's repeated assurance about the nature of God and about our own natures is simply too much for most of us. It is literally unbearable because to internalise it fully requires that our lives be turned upside down; in essence, it leaves us with no way out. It makes nonsense, for example, of all our notions of reward and punishment and the contractual systems that, as individuals and as communities, we establish to regulate our lives. It does away at a stroke with such notions as hell and purgatory and it is interesting, to say the least, that Julian did not see these places. Julian's understanding of the Passion of Christ and its operation does away, too, with the idea of human beings as divided creatures. Constantly she affirms the integrity of the human personality: 'I saw that our nature is wholly in God', she says. What she terms our substance and our sensuality are joined in union because of Christ's Passion: 'That honourable life in which our Lord Jesus sits is our sensuality in which he is enclosed.'

The devil still has an honourable place in Julian's scheme of things but it is striking that his chief preoccupation seems to be in shaking Julian's trust in her own visions. His activity leads to the appearance of the unsung hero of the 'Showings', namely 'a man of religion' – presumably a priest or monk – to whom Julian states that she has been raving and suffering from hallucinations to the extent of seeing the figure on the cross before her bleeding profusely. The cleric's immediate seriousness and surprise pulls her up short and, just in time, she realises that she is on the point of not believing our Lord God! The devil, it is clear, is intent on making her devalue her experience and on driving her away from her perception of the true nature of God and of her own being. It seems to me that the debt we owe to that unknown priest or monk is incalculable. He was, incidentally, a man with a fine sense of humour for he 'laughed aloud and heartily' and his subsequent seriousness was thereby all the more powerful. The devil, according to Julian, is often best vanquished through humour and contempt and she succeeds in reducing him to a rather pathetic figure who can be sent packing through ridicule. Julian clearly loved laughter and she saw heaven as a place of much merrymaking. She would, I believe, have endorsed Meister Eckhart's reflection on the Trinity:

> Do you want to know
> What goes on in the core of the Trinity?
> I will tell you.
> In the core of the Trinity
> the Father laughs
> and gives birth to the Son.
> The Son laughs back at the Father
> and gives birth to the Spirit.
> The whole Trinity laughs
> and gives birth to us.

(Fox, 1983, p. 129)

The unknown cleric, Julian's parish priest, who comes to her in her grave sickness, her beloved even Christians to whom she refers constantly, the blessed saints – especially Mary, the Lord's mother – and those who have sinned grievously like Mary Magdalen, Peter and her contemporary John of Beverly – all these constitute for Julian the community of Holy Church of which she writes that it 'was never broken, nor ever will be without end.' And yet there is no escaping the underlying tension that Julian experiences as she attempts to relate the truth and meaning of her visions to many of the doctrines and practices of the Church of her day. Sometimes the tension cannot be resolved and she is content to let paradoxes remain as mysteries that will only be illuminated when the blessed Trinity performs a 'deed in the last day'. Her expressed submission to the Church is therefore no abject capitulation but rather one made on her own terms – yet another reason for ensuring that her book was for private circulation only! Indeed, her vision of the Church seems to be one where all men and women acknowledge their common membership of the body of Christ and know that they are all the darlings of God. She goes so far as to state that the blood of our own beloved Mother will be sprinkled on us all and that we shall all be healed gently in the course of time. 'From this sweet and gentle operation', she says, 'He will never cease or desist, until all his beloved children are born and brought to birth.' This is a breath-taking vision of the whole of humanity throughout all time and all ages being brought back home to the loving father and mother and lover who cherishes them infinitely for ever.

The counsellor who listened patiently to the garrulous Margery Kempe had no desire to intervene with gratuitous or pious platitudes. She knew that letting Margery talk about herself was a sure way to bring her back to trust in herself and in God – as long as she was not impeded by adverse judgements or condemnatory looks. I have no doubt that Julian regarded Margery with great compassion and tenderness in the manner that she believed God regards us all and that, held in this loving regard, Margery was enabled, through self-exploration, to find her way back to her own soul. I often think about Julian's eyes and the message they transmitted to all who sought her help. Those eyes must have spoken the words that for me sum up the radical, revolutionary and utterly transforming knowledge that resulted from Julian's intimacy with her Lord and lover.

> Whether we are moved to know God or our soul, either motion is good and true. God is closer to us than our own soul, for he is the foundation on which our soul stands and he is the mean which keeps the substance and the sensuality together, so that they will never separate. For our soul sits in God in true rest, and our soul stands in God in sure strength, and our soul is naturally rooted in God in endless love. And therefore if we want to have knowledge

of our soul, and communion and discourse with it, we must seek
in our Lord God in whom it is enclosed.
(The Fifty-sixth Chapter) (Colledge and Walsh, 1978, pp. 288–9)

Perhaps it is now becoming clear why Julian may be seen as perhaps the
most radical psychotherapist there has ever been and why she deserves
to be studied by every aspiring therapist in our own generation. To be
radical is to be concerned with roots and Julian has no doubt where
humanity's true rootedness lies. To the person who is trapped in the fear
of judgement or who has succumbed to the poison of self-hate she
brings news of surpassing wonder. God, she says, is endless love and
there is no judgement and no anger in him. What is more, you and I are
his most precious darlings and nothing we can do will ever alter that
fact. We are safe in God's love and with him we can celebrate the wonder
of our own being, the beauty of our bodies, the glory of our souls. To
those who have been abused by their fellow human beings, even
perhaps by their own parents, she brings the startling news that God is
their most tender Mother and Father since the beginning of time and
will never abandon them. To those who feel alienated and alone and for
whom there is no meaning in life she reveals the tender compassion of
God who created everything for love and preserves it by the same love.
Love is the meaning of the created universe and we are all born that we
may be both lovers and beloved and share in the eternal dance of love
that is the life of the Holy Trinity. There can be no greater belonging than
that and no meaning more sublime. We belong to each other and to the
whole created order and we find our meaning in living out that communion.

The therapist who shares Julian's vision and knows for himself or
herself the reality of which she speaks will look upon those who seek
help with the eyes of God. Tenderness, compassion, understanding and
total lack of judgement, the ability to recognise a beloved son or
daughter or friend or lover of surpassing beauty – these will be the
characteristics of radical psychotherapists who will possess them
because that is how they experience God's love in the citadel of their
own souls. There can be no simulation of such characteristics and the
therapist will be constantly aware that he or she cannot for one moment
deliberately risk losing sight of the blessed face of God; the beams of
love must be borne if the therapeutic work is to be accomplished.

It would be tempting to end on that high note of mystical rhetoric,
but I want instead to return to the streets of Norwich in 1993. This, after
all, is Julian's city and it is here that she wrote her book and fulfilled her
counselling ministry. What has this radical psychotherapist to say to her
fellow-citizens today? We may be sure that she would look upon us with
infinite compassion but I am persuaded that she might also be saddened
that a city that has at least 30 times as many inhabitants as it did in her

day remains so ensnared in the coils of a manipulative, power-hungry and destructive world. She would see our dear city populated by many who drag out their lives in the darkness of self-doubt, low self-esteem, self-rejection and depression. She would see the corrosive effects of a political and economic climate that chooses to ignore the weak and despises the vulnerable. She would see thousands of human beings who have been rejected from the moment of conception and others who have known no real human warmth but only betrayal and abuse since their earliest years. She would see thousands of young people who have little hope of finding meaning in their living and working and some who are prepared to risk death from AIDS so desperate is their craving for intimacy and communion. In short she would see a city where people are as ignorant of their true natures as they were in 1415 and where the devil continues to do his best to undermine those few who catch a glimpse of the truth about themselves. It is that truth that the radical psychotherapist from the fourteenth century would wish to proclaim from the steps of the City Hall. To each and every citizen she would say with utter certainty, 'You are the beloved from all eternity and held safe in an embrace that will never let you go.' To the clergy and the counsellors of our city she would speak, I believe, with the utmost tenderness but her question would be direct and solemn. 'Do you truly believe that you are beloved from all eternity?' This is the question which I ask myself daily for I know that when I can answer confidently and trustingly that I do indeed so believe I will have begun to understand the amazing news which Julian brings to her even Christians. What is more, if I can hold fast to the truth that God is all love and that I and all humanity with me constitute his noblest creation, then, and only then, will I have entered the school of radical psychotherapy whose foundress we are met to honour today.

References

Butler-Bowden W (Tr.) (1936) The Book of Margery Kempe. London: Jonathan Cape.
Colledge E, Walsh J (eds) (1978) Julian of Norwich: Showings. New York: Paulist Press.
Fox M (1983) Meditations with Meister Eckhart. Santa Fé, New Mexico: Bear & Company, Inc.

Chapter 18
Foreword to *Sin shall be a Glory* by John Michael Mountney[1]

Ours is an age when more and more people seem to succumb to stress-related illnesses and conditions. Often this is attributed to the frenetic pace of life or to the rapidity of change in the context of a highly mobile society. The human being, it is argued, is simply not made to withstand such constant pressure or to tolerate an existence of almost perpetual transition.

There may be much truth in these perceptions but, as a practising counsellor and psychotherapist, I am inclined to opt for a more complex and in some ways more sinister explanation. I have come to believe that most of us, most of the time, are increasingly aware of being caught up in a fearsome web of guilt and, like Kafka's K, we have no clear grasp either of our crimes or of the court in which we stand convicted.

It is, of course, true that in Great Britain we have recently moved into a punitive 'accountability and achievement culture', where review and appraisal schemes are the order of the day and where everyone seems busily engaged in evaluating someone else or avoiding the adverse judgement of their own evaluators. The basic principle underlying this culture seems to be that everyone is to be assumed incompetent or to be under-performing until proved otherwise. Not surprisingly, such a negative view of humanity has produced systems that are guaranteed to increase anxiety and to exacerbate the fear of failure. Even those who win favourable judgement and seem to thrive on the competitiveness that the systems intentionally engender are prey to dark fears and underlying tensions, for nothing is worse than having to go on being 'very good' or 'excellent' or 'outstanding'. In our apparent enthusiasm for 'raising standards' we have created a climate in which feelings of guilt and personal inadequacy can rapidly assume grotesque proportions.

---

[1]Taken from *Sin Shall be a Glory* by John Michael Mountney published and copyright 1992 by Darton, Longman & Todd Ltd and used by permission of the publishers.

What, it may be asked, has all this to do with another book on Julian of Norwich? I believe that the connection is immediate and profound, for the self-rejection and guilt feelings nourished by the accountability culture only flourish so monstrously because the psychological ground is already efficiently tilled and prepared in the souls of men and women. In the closing decade of an apparently 'secular' epoch it is clear that, given half a chance, most of us consider ourselves, in the words of the Book of Common Prayer, to be 'miserable sinners' who 'have no health in us'. We are, in fact, whether we know it or not, prisoners of a harsh judgemental theology that has God the eternal Judge seated upon his throne condemning us to hell because we have committed the unforgivable sin. If this seems an exaggeration then you have never sat in the psychotherapist's chair nor perhaps met one of the thousands of people who cannot cross the threshold of their parish church because they deem themselves 'not good enough'.

At such a time, when the ravages of the perverse messages of condemnation, inculcated by a guilt-inducing Church, have bitten deep into the collective unconscious of secularised men and women, Julian's Revelations of Divine Love need to be proclaimed urgently and with authority. In this book, Michael Mountney does just that. As a priest and Warden of the Julian Shrine in Norwich he knows only too well the tangles and torments of those caught up in self-rejection and self-condemnation and so he brings before us Julian's healing insights into the nature of God and of his unconditional love and acceptance of all his creatures. He reminds us, too, of Julian's glimpses into the infinite tenderness of God, whereby, in his sight, we do not fall even when we sin most grievously.

This book, then, does not attempt to evade our reality, for Julian had no doubt that we are sinners and are prone to sin continually. Her revelations point us, however, to the greater reality that 20 centuries of Christianity seem not yet to have fully revealed let alone to have implanted deep in the hearts and minds of men and women. The God of whom Julian speaks loves us not despite our sinfulness but in our sinfulness. What is more, his love is so great that it is not in his nature to forgive for to forgive would be to assume a prior accusation and condemnation of which Julian sees no sign.

My hope is that this soul-loving book will not only bring assurance and deep affirmation to Christian pilgrims on their journey, but will also touch the lives of those who, while they are consciously outside the Christian Church, are the unwitting victims of a punitive God who has never existed and never will.

Chapter 19
Happiness in Relationships[1]

Tonight I want to say some very simple things that are nonetheless, I believe, profound in their implications. As I write I have just come off the phone – a long distance call from the South of France, the caller a young woman on the verge of self-destruction who has suddenly been abandoned by her lover. A few days ago she was supremely happy in her relationship – now she is caught up in the most unutterable despair and does not know if she can continue to live. Throughout the world at this moment her plight is replicated by countless individuals whose relationships have plunged them into perhaps the most appalling hell that human beings can know. What goes on in these situations? Why is it that we humans spend so much of our lives in apparently agonising relationships that cause us untold suffering?

My young friend in France is perhaps not untypical. This is not the first time she has been abandoned. She has experienced the acute pain of rejection before and knows its horrors. Right now she feels worthless; the departure of her lover invalidates her at the core of her being. It is as if his rejection of her induces a most annihilating self-rejection of which she is the agent: she now sees herself as useless, unlovable, without meaning, fit for nothing and for no one. Her attitude towards herself is modelled on what she interprets her lover's attitude to be towards her. But the pain goes deeper even than that: while experiencing herself as worthless she is at the same time conscious that she is full of love. Her heart cries out for and bleeds for the beloved – she, the unlovable, worthless one – is ablaze with a love which burns and consumes her but cannot cast light or warmth for others. In short, her love, which is immense, is destructive; it achieves nothing but her own immolation on the altar of despair.

---

[1]This paper was originally delivered at the Fifth Professional Holiday held at The Old Rectory, Great Melton, Norwich, 23–27 September 1988.

It is in these stark and agonising predicaments that we can see revealed two fundamental truths about the human condition. Firstly, we see that we depend upon others for our sense of worth and conviction that we are beloved and desirable beings. Secondly, we see that we have within us untold potential for loving which needs channels for its expression. If there is nowhere for this love to find an outlet then it turns against us and fuels the fires of self-hate.

If we accept these two truths, then many things follow. It becomes evident, for example, that from the moment of our conception we need the repeated and continuing affirmation from others that our basic nature is loveable and desirable. This will be conveyed by attitude, by word, by touch, by all manner of visible and invisible means – or, as is mostly the case – it will not be conveyed or it will be communicated only partially or intermittently. A rarity therefore is the man or woman who is so surrounded in this way by grace abounding that he or she comes to know the fundamental belovedness of his or her nature. For most of us most of the time this is a far cry from the feelings we have about ourselves which are of inadequacy, failure or even of evil and corruption.

The concept of ourselves as potential lovers of immense capacity is perhaps even more alien to our everyday experience. We are usually overwhelmed by feelings of the tragic insufficiency of our loving: we are aghast at the imponderable suffering in the world and retreat into frightened passivity. Unless, of course, we fall in love – that strange, magical, psychotic experience – which shows us that, to our astonishment, we have so much love that we do not know what to do with it all. Unfortunately all too often we cannot cope with the infinite resources that are revealed in ourselves: we squander them, we surrender to their immensity and as a result the object of our love can feel drowned, imprisoned, oppressed, suffocated. It is our very loving that drives the beloved away by its sheer power and the insistence of its demands.

What a doleful scenario! Is there any hope that it can be changed? Could it be that we might find a way of living together in the world that enables us to celebrate our belovedness and our capacity to love – a way of being, in short, which might actually lead to happiness in our relationships? I am crazy and idealistic enough to imagine that such a possibility might not be altogether beyond our grasp. These occasions at the Old Rectory provide a unique opportunity for indulging in quasi-Utopian dreams, so here goes.

Much of this is somewhat Pascalian. Blaise Pascal, you remember, was a remarkable seventeenth century French mathematician and Christian philosopher who decided that the only sane way to live was to live as if God existed. If God did not exist then nothing was lost but if he did then the potential benefits were so enormous that only a fool would refuse the wager. What I wish in similar vein to explore now is the implications of living as if:

- I am infinitely desirable and lovable while needing the affirmation of others to keep me true to my nature.
- I have vast resources for loving and need to find channels for such loving.

Let us look at the first assertion. I shall live as if I am infinitely desirable and lovable. Clearly this has massive implications for my attitude towards myself. In brief, I shall love myself despite all the evidence of which I might be conscious that runs counter to the notion of my desirability. I shall cherish myself and endow myself with deep respect. I shall care for my body and learn to love it even if it is not as shapely as I should wish or as beautiful as the woman's who lives next door. I shall pay attention to my own thoughts and feelings and see them as important and not deride them. I shall be kind to myself in all manner of ways which does not mean indulging myself or being slovenly and lazy for such attitudes are not ultimately kind at all - they spoil and sell short the person I am. In brief, I shall cultivate an internal lover of me and give him or her all possible assistance.

This internal lover of me, however, has need of companions in the task. The internal lover looks to others who can also be relied upon to cherish me. But where are such people, you may ask? Perhaps my parents constantly criticise me, my peers tease or ignore me, my lovers abuse me. There are no companions for my internal lover and so he or she will rapidly give up the unequal struggle and leave me in the clutches of self-hate. If this is the case, dear friend, then you must seek assiduously for those who will cherish you. Certainly you may have to leave those who deny your desirability or threaten to destroy your internal lover or even to forbid his appearance. If you really mean to live as if you are infinitely desirable you cannot allow yourself to remain in the power of those who seem bent on convincing you of your imperfection, inadequacy or corruption. That may sound a tough message and, indeed, it is. Of course, you may discover a satisfactory compromise. It may prove possible to go on living with those punitive parents or that condemnatory husband because your internal lover has been able to find a true companion somewhere else – a new friend who cherishes or affirms, a counsellor or therapist perhaps, a priest who accepts unreservedly. Curiously enough when this happens and you grow stronger in the knowledge of your own desirability – the 'as if' is replaced by a conviction of what truly is – so the parents seem less punitive, the husband less harsh in his condemnation. The chances are, of course, that they have changed not a jot but you are now less vulnerable to their attacks. Sometimes, however, the process proves somewhat different. As your internal lover finds a new companion in the task of affirming your desirability so you become progressively more appalled at the hostility of those with whom you live or work. You have tasted a new world and you can no longer tolerate the old. Then you must depart and leave the punishers and bearers of condemnation to find other victims. Your internal lover rejoices as progressively he finds himself in more congenial company. Does this all sound very immoral or hedonistic? Do I sound like the devil tempting wives and husbands to leave their spouses or children to abandon parents? If I do then remember the words of Christ who challenged spouses to leave their partners and children to quit their parents for His sake. What did He mean? For me He was throwing down the gauntlet to those who truly desired to enter the service of Love. If we do not seek to accept and affirm our own desirability then we throw God's acceptance and love of us back in His face. It is our obligation to seek by all possible means to arrive at a self-love that acknowledges that we are children of God and therefore carry within us the seed of divinity.

I am writing now on the 6.30 from Liverpool Street and I have just finished a good meal – soup, salmon, Norfolk turkey cordon bleu and much cheese. I have had a rather wretched day and a tiring journey to London, an exhausting committee meeting, no lunch to speak of. I decided to cherish myself: dinner with gin and wine. I am a little drunk: I have spent perhaps too much money. I am, however, full of gratitude that I have sufficient cash to make such a luxury possible. I rejoice in the memories that have flooded me during the meal – of people much loved with whom I have dined in the past, of marvellous evenings in Italy with those who loved me with a totally unpossessive affection, of my wife who has always allowed me to be me despite the pain, of boys and girls whom I have introduced to the life of holy hedonism and who have rewarded me with their warmest embraces: my joy is such that I am close to tears.

But, remember, there is another side to this coin. What is the other basic assumption of my 'as if' challenge? I must live as if I have vast resources for loving and need to find channels for that loving. What does it mean to do that? Supremely it means that I must trust my empathic self. I must believe that I have the capacity to enter the worlds of other human beings and to dwell there in such a way that they feel my closeness and understanding. Nobody is beyond my reach. Can I really act as if that were true? Can I act as if I can come alongside the football hooligan, the fascist, the starving peasant of Bangladesh, the company man, the cardinal and the prostitute. Can I believe, in short, that I am godlike, that I have divine potential?

And so we come to the crunch of the matter. Have you ever tried to unravel the doctrine of the Holy Trinity – one of the most astonishing concepts ever given to the mind of humanity? There we have mirrored the perfect relationship, the relationship where happiness is assured. In that doctrine is represented a relationship where we see what happens when loving flows without encumbrance between persons. Let us put it into the context of human relating. Tom knows that he is desirable and that he has the inherent capacity to enter the world of Lucy and to be fully with her there. Lucy for her part knows that she is desirable and is therefore able to open herself to Tom's love without fear. Should he fail her or abandon her she will be sad, distraught but not annihilated. She will know in the deepest part of her being that the failure or the abandonment is the outcome of unrealised potential, of incompleteness, of not yet wholeness rather than a sign that she is worthless or that he is utterly malevolent or that the human race is doomed. Father and Son are God and can therefore trust the operation of the Holy Spirit: Tom and Lucy are children of God, they are made for deification, and therefore take the risk of trusting themselves to each other knowing that whatever the pain, suffering and failure there lies the inescapable truth that ultimately they are members one of another. Here then is the road to happiness in relationships and what is more amazing is that as a species we are walking along it even if as yet we only momentarily glimpse the destination.

Chapter 20
Time: Friend or Enemy?[1]

As I sit to write this paper I am immediately confronted by the very issue that the paper itself purports to address. I have an hour before lunch and during that time I wish to make substantial inroads into the topic so that later this week I can take up the paper again secure in the knowledge that I have at least made a good start.

I could, of course, choose to be defeated at the outset. I could simply say, for example, that an hour is far too short a time to be able to produce anything of any interest or merit and I should simply wait for a more propitious opportunity when I have several hours stretching in front of me. In short, I could allow this one hour of time to defeat me, to reduce me to an ignominious heap of ineffectiveness and spend the next hour disconsolately thumbing through journals looking for inspiration.

That, of course, is what countless students do every day of the year in our institutions of learning. They are working on all sorts of assumptions most of which are probably only half conscious and almost all of which are unlikely to be articulated. Here are a few of them.

- Something of worth cannot be produced in a short time.
- The brain cannot be programmed to work at different speeds.
- Experience is a dubious resource and other people's considered treatises are of far greater importance.
- We are the victims of past behaviour and cannot choose new ways of being.
- It is intolerably painful to think rapidly.

In all these assumptions there is the hidden idea that time is some kind of absolute that determines or controls what we can do and the quality

---

[1]This paper was originally delivered at the Fourth Professional Holiday held at The Old Rectory, Great Melton, Norwich, 18–22 September 1987.

of our achievement. It is seldom, I believe, that we consider the possibility that we can actually control time rather than it controlling us – that is, it is seldom that we can conceive ourselves as being essentially creatures whose natural habitat is not timebound.

Despite ourselves, we sometimes glimpse this possibility. We dream and are astounded that we have apparently lived half a lifetime within a couple of minutes. We daydream on a hot summer's afternoon and feel ourselves plunged back into memories of infancy. Perhaps, like Proust, we eat a madeleine or smell a smell and are transported to another place and to another epoch. We may even have the misfortune of nearly drowning and find ourselves reviewing our total existence within a matter of seconds. But we don't take such things very seriously: we tell ourselves that they are only dreams or daydreams or freak occurrences. They can tell us nothing about the hard reality of conscious living where an hour is an unchangeable and implacable prison.

How strange that we should so readily accept defeat. In exams, of course, some of us actually change our tune. We move from the angry assertion that nobody can possibly say anything worth saying in 40 minutes in response to the complex questions beloved of examiners to a position where we are willing to pull out all the stops (interesting metaphor that – makes one feel like a magnificently powerful organ). Then our hand flashes across the page at the speed of lightning: the thoughts tumble over one another, our passive vocabulary springs amazingly to life and after half an hour we have covered six or seven pages of A4 paper. We can't believe it, of course, and are certain that we have written a load of drivel – quality is by definition impossible because it was, after all, only half an hour. The effort is considerable because we are unaccustomed to flying along like this; we have to concentrate like nobody's business and it is all very unusual. But caution goes to the wind and we hurry on, willing for once to let ourselves have our heads and not to pause too long to wonder whether the examiners will pass a favourable or an adverse judgement.

Once, 20-odd years ago, I enjoyed myself immensely by demonstrating to a group of 25 students that they could learn a vast amount in two minutes. I gave them all a copy of the same book and told them they had two minutes to read it before taking an examination on its content. They went wild with activity and devoured the book with startling application: in the examination they demonstrated that they had not only grasped the book's main thesis but were even able to produce some illustrative data of some of the central issues. I challenged them to consider whether or not the knowledge they had gained under such unusual circumstances was somehow illicit, invalid, spurious because, after all, they had gained it in only two minutes. Most of them were delightfully confused; they felt both elated and guilty that they had acquired so much in so little time.

I would suggest that most of us are far too obsequious in our attitude to time. We allow it to become a major factor in our attitude to ourselves and in our assessment of our lives. We do not start from the assumption that time is there to serve us if only we will befriend it. We are not born to be time's prisoners. The trouble begins, I suspect, as soon as we start worrying about tomorrow to the detriment of today. Perhaps it is not going to an absurd length to suggest that we stop living as soon as we start worrying at some level about dying. Certainly if we perceive death as the ultimate enemy we shall see the passing hours and years as the advance infantry of our insidious foe. John Donne had the right idea when he challenged Death not to be so proud. For eternal creatures time is relative, often an irrelevance and death is not 'mighty and dreadful' but an incident along the way.

Gosh – that's where I've got to in less than an hour, actually, because my lunch guest has arrived a quarter of an hour early. How splendid to have bumped up against John Donne again and, as I write this last sentence before my aperitif, I find myself in the Lake District with Wordsworth and sharing his Intimations of Immortality, which are in many ways a reflection on the despairing attitude to Time that I am attempting to question and even to subvert in this paper. Wordsworth's imagery of the prison house takes up once more the theme of imprisonment, of being caught in a kind of temporal straitjacket. When the imprisonment is complete everything has faded into the light of common day. There is an important link here. It would seem, according to Wordsworth, that with the clanging of the gate of our temporal gaol we are also finally deprived of the ability to see wonders, to be at home in heaven. Is there not an awful truth here? Once we have accepted Time as our Lord and Master then we are deprived of the gift of awe and wonder. So often we glimpse this sad outcome when we are in the company of small children. They wish to pause a while to contemplate something to our eyes apparently insignificant and boring: they are fascinated by a flower or a pebble or a worm. It is rare, however, for us adults to have much patience with such contemplation: we quickly become impatient and wish to get on in order to accomplish the next part of our programme. 'We cannot stay here all day' we irritably comment and drag the wretched child away from its musings. We have dealt another blow at the faculty of awe and wonder. But why should we not spend all day in awe and wonder and musing? When we think back on childhood I would not mind betting that many of us have memories of long summer days and holidays that seemed to go on for ever. We had the ability then to live at the rhythm of eternity.

Of course Wordsworth himself struggled valiantly to resist the imprisonment of which he speaks in the Immortality Ode. He knew that if he could keep properly in touch with nature, if he could continue to cherish such communion, then he would still be free. And yet despite his determination he could lament:

> There was a time when meadow, grove, and stream,
> The earth, and every common sight,
>> To me did seem
>> Apparelled in celestial light,
> The glory and the freshness of a dream.
> It is not now as it has been of yore;—
>> Turn wheresoe'er I may.
>> By night or day,
> The things which I have seen I now can see no more.

(Intimations of Immortality from Recollections of Early
Childhood)

He never really capitulated though. How could he in his Lakeland home? Hills and lakes and the changing seasons put our puny anxieties into perspective. There is great truth here. If we believe that we have fallen into the clutches of malevolent Time, the harbinger of death rather than the symbol of eternity, then we need to restore our contact with the created world.

We need to lift up our eyes to the hills, we need to hear again the gentle lap of waves on the seashore, we need to walk barefoot in the grass of the meadow. When I was a teacher at Eastbourne College I used to go out sometimes very late at night and walk along the promenade or stand staring out to sea. Very often I was not alone: I would see – and then pretend not to see – one of my pupils who had somehow escaped down a drainpipe from his dormitory. He, too, would be reconnecting his soul to the created world of which he was a part in order to salvage a life which for the most part was ruled by bells and the pressure of the next compulsory activity.

There is a more sinister side to this story, though. If the boy had been discovered or if I had turned traitor and reported him then he would have been in serious trouble. In the eyes of the boarding school authorities he was committing a crime and would have to be punished. He was guilty.

Often, it seems to me, it is precisely feelings of guilt or potential guilt that make it well-nigh impossible for many of us to befriend time. We are so obsessed with the fear of wasting time that all too often we never relax into embracing it. I know this conflict within myself only too well. Sometimes at the end of a day I find myself cross-examining myself to discover how useful I have been, how constructive. 'What', I ask myself, 'have I achieved today?' We are moving into a phase in our national life when such neurosis is encouraged and exacerbated by the prevailing ethos. Concepts like accountability, cost-effectiveness, appraisal all point to a preoccupation with the proper use of time when proper usually means something to do with the organisation's profitability. Wasting time means not making money or not achieving tangible and measurable objectives. And so it is that managers work 80-hour weeks and refuse to take holidays and members of the helping professions collapse with exhaustion while their clients continue their merry dance undismayed. What utter insanity and yet to risk becoming sane brings with it so often the burden of intolerable guilt. 'I ought to be working harder.' 'I mustn't let the firm down.' 'I must win my supervisor's approval.' 'I must show that I am tough, resilient and indestructible.' Dear God, what sort of life is that?

I have often spoken before of my old friend and mentor George Lyward and of his wonderful therapeutic community at Finchden Manor. George believed that many of his deeply disturbed adolescent clients were the victims of time schedules, of fixed objectives, of the imposition of the adult prison-house where everything had faded into the light of common day. And so it was that at Finchden, Time the Enemy, the harbinger of death was banished and Time the Friend, the Lover of Life reigned supreme. What joy that was! It meant that what really mattered was truly attended to. If I was tired I could sleep on and nobody would be banging on my door demanding that I be about my duties. If I sensed that someone wanted my company for an hour or two then I was free to be with that person. If I wanted to be alone then I could wander off and enjoy my solitude. The truly amazing thing about all this was that it did not lead to selfishness and separation but to the profoundest sense of connectedness and community. Meals were always cooked – if sometimes late – jobs got done, pets were well looked after, persons relaxed into being and at long last could find the possibility of fulfilment. I believe, looking back on it, that there was another profound reason why Time the Enemy could be so powerfully banished. George Lyward himself had faced much despair and disintegration in his own life and most of the boys at Finchden had looked death in the face – some had indeed attempted suicide. In a strange way, therefore, almost everyone there had contemplated the possibility of his own extinction and were no longer afraid of that possibility. I am reminded of words of Metropolitan Anthony Bloom: 'Death is the touchstone of our attitude to life. People who are afraid of death are afraid of life. It is impossible not to be afraid of life with all its complexity and dangers if one is afraid of death.'

In a strange way and for the most tragic reasons I believe that many of the young people at Finchden had actually faced death at the outset. For them, therefore, it was not only possible but imperative that they embrace life and in order to do so they required the banishment of Time the Enemy.

It is also, I am sure, significant that Finchden Manor was a place of great hilarity. Something funny always seemed to be happening and there was much laughter even amidst grave personal suffering. When Time the Enemy is in the ascendant there is, of course, little room for laughter. Laughing is a waste of time diverting attention from the serious business – and yet laughter is essential to life. I am always delighted to know from Mother Julian that in heaven people are 'right merry'.

I have not stopped often to pause during the writing of this paper: in some sense, then, it is something of a stream of consciousness effort. And yet I feel that certain themes emerge clearly enough. Let me attempt to summarise:

- Most of us most of the time are slaves of time rather than its masters. We have many false assumptions about the relationship between time and the creation or the experience of something worthwhile. But a great poem can be written in five minutes and a life changed in half a second. We even allow time to convince us that we cannot think or work quickly instead of facing the less palatable truth that we do not care to engage in the pain of thinking and working with intensity.
- Death needs to be faced if we are to embrace life, take risks and not be forever anxious about wasting time and making mistakes.
- We allow the prison of time to separate us from each other and from the companionship of the created world. We are part of a created whole and we need to be constantly reminded of this by nourishing ourselves with the wonders of the natural world. Time the Enemy blunts our sense of awe and wonder. Time the Friend bids us stand and stare and feed upon the beauty of the earth.
- We need to be acutely aware of the insidious way in which our present society, with its emphasis on efficiency and profitability, is creating the perfect environment for Time the Enemy to wreak havoc.
- Love and laughter often go hand-in-hand and neither can flourish in a tight schedule where all that matters is achieving targets and sacrificing all on the altar of high standards.

In an important way I believe that this series of Professional Holidays and this very place point to a spirited attempt to welcome Time the Friend. I believe that the English have shown enormous sagacity in this matter by inventing and cherishing the game of cricket. Despite some of the latest innovations in the game, which are to be deplored, cricket can still never really be hurried. Batsmen still walk to the crease, they still pat down imaginary bumps, they still gaze round at all and sundry before settling down to receive a ball. Bowlers still walk slowly back to the beginning of their run, they still rub the ball on their trouser leg, they still pause before they erupt into movement. Hours can pass with little to disturb the peace except the click of ball on bat or the cry of an expectant wicket-keeper who attempts to manipulate a sleepy umpire into an l.b.w. decision. And then suddenly everything can happen in the space of half a minute. Time itself luxuriates in a cricket match – Time the Friend and Time the Enemy declare a truce until stumps are drawn. Where there's cricket there's hope and laughter, too.

PART IV
The Sermons of a Person-centred Counsellor

Introduction

I am fairly confident in asserting that this final part of the book is unique in the literature of person-centred therapy. The very idea of a person-centred counsellor preaching sermons will be abhorrent to those who mistakenly see preaching as an activity focused on telling others what to do; the decision to publish such aberrations will seem even more bizarre.

For me, however, these addresses are significant for a number of reasons. In the first place, I am moved by the trust placed in me by those who issued me with the invitations to preach. The position of the preacher is a powerful one and it is tempting to abuse such power. What is more, these sermons were delivered in places of some renown and often on very special occasions. The pulpits of cathedrals and prestigious Cambridge colleges are not regularly put at the disposal of lay persons who have no ecclesiastical legitimacy for being there. Those who invited me were taking a risk and knew that they would have to live with the consequences. Secondly, the task of preaching a sermon invariably forces me to re-examine my beliefs and to strip myself, as far as this is ever possible, of self-deception. These sermons, then, are no exercise in rhetoric or theological exegesis. They are my honest and sometimes painful attempt to be true to my own experience while honouring and respecting the wisdom of the Christian tradition. I like to believe that, in this respect, I am faithful to the example of Julian of Norwich although I am thankfully aware that for me to misjudge the situation would not lead to being burnt in the Lollards pit as it might well have done for her. Thirdly, I am aware that running through almost all these sermons there are certain themes that are of central importance to me and that have often constituted the terrain on which my life as a therapist and my commitment as a Christian have entered into the most intense dialogue. The personhood of Jesus, the unconditionality of God's love, the

131

interconnectedness of all humanity, the meaning of eternity, the communion of saints, the sacredness of the body, the sacrament of sexuality, the vulnerability of the lover, the challenge of intimacy, the provisionality of revealed truth – all these find some expression in these seven sermons and, together with *Behold the Man*, they constitute a kind of testimony of what it has meant and continues to mean for me to be a member of two 'communities of faith'. I have also not forgotten that as I left the pulpit of Leicester Cathedral on World AIDS Day, 1991, I wept.

Chapter 21
A Sermon Preached in the Chaplaincy of the University of East Anglia, Norwich, All Saints Day 1981

Almighty God, you have knit together your elect into one communion and fellowship in the mystical body of your Son. Give us grace so to follow your blessed saints in all virtuous and godly living, that we may come to those unspeakable joys which you have prepared for those who truly love you.

(Collect for All Saints Day)

This morning's collect is a most remarkable affair and I want to talk for a few minutes about it. More particularly I want to focus on the words 'one communion and fellowship in the mystical body of your Son'. You will remember that we are assured by the collect that it is precisely into this mystical body that we are all 'knit together'.

It is my habit to write sermons and articles in my head while I am walking about the place doing other things. If I cut you dead when we next pass each other on the campus please be merciful. It so happened that I was engaged in writing this sermon while waiting for the 8 o'clock to London last Monday morning. I was also reading *The Times* and was therefore much amused to spot a small headline at the foot of the first page that said 'Corpus Christi to admit women'. This news item about the decision of a Cambridge College to admit female students and fellows seemed marvellously apt to my embryonic thoughts on today's sermon. Good Heavens! The body of Christ to admit women in 1982 – progress indeed! Already I could see the announcements: Corpus Christi College: elected into a tutorial fellowship, Miss Zoe Ossenpfeffer currently lecturer in management science at the Teeside Polytechnic; Organ scholar: Penelope Jane Digby-Harcourt of the Cheltenham Ladies College. Which reminds me that the collect refers to us as 'the elect' – it is the elect who are so knitted together that they are 'one communion and fellowship in the mystical body'. We are all chosen.

All Saints Day is the perfect occasion for reflecting on these issues. For me this November festival conjures up memories of boyhood zeal, getting out of bed at an unearthly hour to attend Sung Mass – yes sung and with clouds of incense – at 6.30 in the morning. No food in one's stomach produced a tendency to faintness but this I recall could be turned to mystical advantage. An icy morning, fog, and a cold church and yet the light of many candles and singing and rejoicing at the extraordinary thought of the countless millions of saints, known and unknown, who had gone before. Such a setting could induce a marvellous reverie on the Saints. There were my favourites, of course – then as now – like St John the Apostle whom I always thought of as the symbol of eternal youth although he is supposed to have died a natural death at a very old age; Mary Magdalen because I was sure she was very beautiful and because she dared to love imperfectly; Francis of Assisi because of the amazing strength of his gentleness; John Henry Newman because he wrote English so beautifully including hymns that I was sure the angels had added to their repertoire. Nowadays, of course, I should add Julian of Norwich because she is the most stunningly avant-garde theologian I have ever stumbled upon and she lives right here in this marvellous city.

Looking back on those formative years of mine in the period after the Second World War I am enormously thankful that I learned to breathe in that somewhat rarefied air. All unknown to me I was learning to live in eternity or perhaps, to put it better, I was learning that we are already living in eternity. These people I have been talking about, John, Mary, Francis, John Henry, Julian, are part of me and it's fun to find out what they are thinking and feeling – always bearing in mind, of course, that they have probably grown up quite a bit since they were knocking around in bodily form in this particular bit of eternity. I can never understand, incidentally, why some people get in such a lather about praying to the saints. To me it's simply a question of taking full advantage of my membership of the mystical body. I like having such friends to chat with and when I'm chatting with them it's obvious that God is in on the conversation because if He wasn't I couldn't possibly be doing such a crazy thing and they wouldn't be saints to talk to anyway.

What amuses me as I think back on it is the comparatively poor opinion I had 30 odd years ago of my contemporary fellow Christians. The vicar, I recall, was a very difficult chap. It was rumoured that he had been in love with a famous singer called Anne Ziegler but she had gone off and married another famous singer called Webster Booth. Ever since that time the vicar had become a misogynist and put much of his energy into being President of the local branch of the Society of King Charles the Martyr. The Churchwarden's wife was called Miriam and made her own hats, which were quite unspeakable. One of the sidesmen was arrested for indecent exposure in the city and nearly went to gaol. They were a very motley crew and it is only now, I think, that I realise they were quite magnificent. Most of them had survived the rigours of the war and had suffered a lot in the process. Some were mentally ill, others had the barest minimum in the way of formal education. They certainly were not on the whole particularly virtuous. But I realise now that they were all caught up in something far greater than themselves and were trying to find their place in it all. What is more they were arrogant enough and humble enough to claim their rights as children of God.

Nowadays I think I'm a bit better at recognising the saints who are there under my very nose. It becomes much easier when you begin to take seriously the fact that Our Lord dwells in all of us even though sometimes he may be ever so hidden. We are the mystical body of Christ precisely because we are the place of His in-dwelling. For this reason we are knit together into one communion and fellowship whether we like it or not together with all those whom he has 'elected' to be fellows of His company – that is to say with all our bothers and sisters who are part of the human family, living and departed.

And so the really important question, once we have accepted that we are part of the mystical body whether we know it or not, is how best to make use of this enormous privilege. I believe that the answer lies in openness. If I want to explore the profound implications of my member-ship of the mystical body I need to be open to the Christ who is within me and to the Christ who is within my fellow human beings. This, it seems to me, is where all spirituality begins – with our ordinary relation-ships and the connections that we make.

Spirituality is a becoming, a dynamic process and so it leads to mystery. We cannot know what there is to be known about ourselves or others except by exploring our possibilities through exercising our ability to be open to each other, and that process is spirituality. I am a mystery to myself and we are all mysteries to one another. But in that mystery God dwells and invites us to relate without fear so that through knowing ourselves and each other more fully we may come close to Him. There was a time when I found it easier to be open to those who no longer walked this earth because with them I did not go in fear of judge-ment. Perhaps it is like that for some of you and, if it is so, celebrate the Communion of Saints that embraces the living and the more fully living. My prayer would be, however, that in the fullness of time we may all come to recognise our common membership of the mystical body and be filled with the yearning to love each other as we are loved by Him who chooses the heart of each one of us as His most blessed home.

Chapter 22
A Sermon on St Paul preached in the Chapel of Trinity College, Cambridge, 26 February 1984

My knowledge now is partial. (1 Cor. 13.12)

St Paul believed in radical change. For him the Crucifixion and Resurrection of Jesus Christ had already changed everything. What is more, scarcely anyone has ever changed the course of history as much as Paul himself. A man who believes in change and who is himself an impassioned change-agent must inevitably evoke violent reactions in others. And it is this that Paul continues to do today. In a world that is being transformed and changed beyond recognition by the inexorable advance of technology, Paul stands as a beacon of hope that other and deeper changes are possible in the hearts and minds of men and women. But how he is loved and hated, this man who proclaimed total transformation. For some he is the first and most potent corrupter of a vital, true religion that has never recovered from his meddling, while for others he is the greatest theologian of all time.

I should be surprised if previous preachers in this series have not emphasised the need to understand Paul within the context of the world and culture of his time. Most importantly, they are likely to have drawn attention to the fact that Paul believed that he was living in the closing days before the end of the world. There may be some in this Chapel who will not find it difficult to empathise with Paul in this respect. Indeed, if you believe that we are unlikely to survive to the end of this century you are already to some extent standing in Pauline shoes. Does such a belief wonderfully concentrate your mind as it does his? For him it meant devoting all his time and energy to what was really important – namely the transformation of men and women through the proclamation of the gospel and the doing of the will of God. And he was often clear that these vital activities were not likely to be advanced through sex and the desires of the flesh.

We need not perhaps go as far as Havelock Ellis who castigated Paul as a morbid neuropath with a warped personality who 'trampled on nature when it came his way and for the rest never saw it'. On the other hand I do not think it possible to deny that Paul's attitude to sex often seems hostile and that he frequently exhibits an almost general contempt for the flesh and fleshly things. What else can we make of such jolly admonitions as: 'It is a good thing for a man to have nothing to do with women; but because there is so much immorality, let each man have his own wife and each woman her own husband?' In other words, remain bachelors and celibate but if the social pressures are such that this is impossible for you to cope with, get married and at least keep your sexual activity contained. Paul even stresses the point: 'To the unmarried and to widows, I say this: it is a good thing if they stay as I am myself, but if they cannot control themselves they should marry. Better be married than burn with vain desire.'

It is possible of course, to argue that Paul's pejorative attitude is merely a response to 'an emergency'. If the world is about to come to an end then sex should be avoided or at the very least kept firmly within tight limits. After all it was common in Jewish circles to suspend normal activities in times of great crisis: during a holy war men gave up not only sex but also – and perhaps more incredibly – business dealings. I don't believe myself, however, that Paul's hostility to sex can be attributed wholly to his belief in the imminence of the Second Coming. The harshness of his condemnation of sexual offenders seems too marked for that and the tone of his general pronouncements on the flesh is scarcely reassuring. 'Flesh and blood can never possess the kingdom of God' he says and again in the famous (or notorious) passage in the first chapter of Romans he castigates deviant sexual practices with unrestrained vehemence. 'God has given them up to shameful passions. Their women have exchanged natural intercourse for unnatural and their men in turn, giving up natural relations with women, burn with lust for one another; males behave indecently with males and are paid in their own persons the fitting wage of such perversion.'

All of this makes depressing reading even granted that Paul's letters emerged out of the context of a licentious cultural climate. Indeed there are those who argue that Paul is a product of the profound spiritualistic dualism that arose in later Greek culture. The soul according to Plato is timeless and immaterial and the senses offer little help in knowing the real world. Sacred love is concerned with the beauties of the soul whereas the body merely provides the occasion for profane love. Sexual activity can therefore have nothing to do with the real existence of the soul but is rather a distraction from it.

To see Paul in this dualistic way is to do him a grave injustice. It is to forget that he is also 'the apostle of love'. It is to forget, too, that it was precisely physical and sexual imagery that he used to describe some of the greatest truths of the faith he proclaimed. John Robinson, the famous Bishop of Woolwich who wrote *Honest to God* and who subsequently became Dean of this college, even wrote a book some 30 years ago entitled *The Body: A Study in Pauline Theology,* in which he maintained that the concept of the body forms the very foundation stone of Paul's theology. Most striking of all is Paul's choice of the union in marriage as a parable of the 'great mystery' that unites Christ to His church – that is to us. We are united to Christ, says Paul, in the way a husband and wife are united – our communion with Him can be dimly grasped by comparing it with the complete union, physical, sexual as well as spiritual, that takes place between a loving husband and wife. Just listen:

> Husbands, love your wives, as Christ also loved the church and gave himself up for it, to consecrate it, cleansing it by water and word, so that he might present the church to himself all glorious, with no stain or wrinkle or anything of the sort, but holy and without blemish. In the same way men also are bound to love their wives, as they love their own bodies. In loving his wife, a man loves himself. For no one ever hated his own body; on the contrary, he provides and cares for it: and that is how Christ treats the church, because it is his body.

This is the apostle of love in full flood and it is clear that he is struggling to express what is for him inexpressible. Love is a mystery, God's love for us the greatest mystery of all. In an even more famous passage about love from which I have taken my text this evening, Paul openly acknowledges his inability to describe the inexpressible 'Now we see only puzzling reflections in a mirror, but then we shall see face to face. My knowledge now is partial; then it will be whole, like God's knowledge of me.'

Paul's admission that his knowledge is partial is for me immensely liberating for it permits me to say with Sydney Carter: 'Shut the Bible up. But then open it up again, DO NOT use it in the way you did before. DO NOT use it as a bludgeon. Do not say I must believe it because it is the word of God: The word of God is in the Bible, said George Fox but the word of God is in you and me as well. The word in the Bible and the word in me must spark and kindle.' Once I can see the Bible like that rather than making an idol of it I am immediately released to see Paul's partial understanding as a remarkable achievement for a man of his time and culture rather than as a permanent obstacle to further understanding. Divine truth is for ever becoming manifest and perhaps there is no sphere in which this is happening more dramatically at present than in the intimate relationships between human beings.

It is to Paul's eternal credit that, despite the deep ambivalence towards sex that pervades much of his thought, there are moments when he glimpses that sex for human beings is a language of love. The connection between sex and love–celebrated gloriously by the writer of the Song of Solomon and then apparently erased from the collective ecclesiastical consciousness – is still in the process of being discovered in our own century. It has had to wait a long time for full acknowledgement but I believe that its hour has now come. Christian thought throughout the centuries has caused endless confusion about human sexuality by its insistence on separating eros from agape and by refusing to allow libido (or epithymia as it used to be called) a look in at all. Time is too short to dwell on the burden of guilt that countless Christian souls have had to endure because of the failure to recognise that our sexuality underpins and informs all our loving. Along with this failure there has often been a total and calamitous denigration of the functions of desire and self love. Only now are Christians beginning to discover that love is indivisible – that self love and other-love are all of one piece – that erotic desire and sacrificial empathy are close companions in the world of intimacy – that sexual orientation is not fundamentally relevant to our divinely-given capacity for communion.

And what of Jesus? He seems to say little on sexual issues but when his words are recorded they insist on the supreme necessity for love and forgiveness in sexual matters as well as in every other area of human life. Perhaps, however, it is not his words that are important but rather his way of life. Touching, embracing, establishing intimacy in a moment of encounter, often surrounded by women, psychologically free to relate to whomever he wished and ultimately exposed naked upon a Cross. Adam hid himself from God because he was naked; Christ, the Second Adam, God incarnate, the word made flesh, was content to be stripped naked for love. He who hung there was fully man, fully physical, fully sexual, whole and holy. And it was Paul who proclaimed that Our Blessed Lord loves us as a husband loves his wife. It is with that image that I would leave you. It is the picture of a contemporary Christ tenderly and lovingly enjoying full sexual union with his beloved. And if that picture is offensive it may be because we believe that sex is unworthy of our Saviour because it is unworthy of us. If that is indeed where we find ourselves then Paul's partial knowledge threatens to remain an obstacle for us rather than the inspiration to discover more. But discover more we must – and if we can, then perhaps we shall find, like Paul, that we are not after all living at five minutes to midnight or, if we are, that when midnight strikes we shall be ready for our divine bridegroom.

Chapter 23
A Sermon preached in Leicester Cathedral on World AIDS Day, Advent Sunday 1991

You are the light of the world (Matthew 5:14)

Success has brought me world idolisation and millions of pounds, but it's prevented me from having the one thing we all need – a loving, ongoing relationship. (Freddie Mercury of 'Queen')

Perhaps each era has its own special form of darkness, its own speciality for extinguishing the human spirit. In a way our present epoch has been curiously unimaginative for the deity who has been presiding for some time now is none other than the old stager 'Mammon' who has waged many successful campaigns down the ages of human history and is an acknowledged expert at darkness creation.

This time round, however, Mammon has deployed new sophisticated weapons that are particularly effective in the crippling of the human spirit. Perhaps the most insidious is a form of indiscriminate artillery shelling known as playing the Market Forces. Market Forces have the effect of depersonalising human beings so that they lose the capacity to relate to each other as persons. Instead they learn to price themselves and each other like so many footballers up for transfer except that the sums involved are in most cases rather paltry. Indeed there are even those who decide that they are worth nothing at all and jump into the rubbish bin and await the refuse collector. Alarmingly, but perhaps predictably under the rule of Mammon, many become skilled at producing 'packages' that are traded around the place like commodities listed in the catalogue of some Supermarket of Life. They often have attractive names, like Knowledge, Security, and Personal Happiness but despite their elegant appearance they seem to lack the mysterious quality of the 'real thing' although the depersonalised shoppers may only be dimly aware of this as they pass through the checkout point.

Light in such a world, populated as it is by characters wearing price-tags and fighting for their corner in the Great Competition, comes from those who resolutely refuse to be objects for barter in the market place. Such people insist on being persons and seeing others as persons too.

This is a hazardous task for it demands a level of vulnerability that, for many, is unthinkable because it remains outside the imaginative scope of a depersonalised being with a price tag. Mercifully, however, such vulnerability can have a transforming power that can bring about – usually at great cost to those concerned – the resurrection of the depersonalised ones. Vulnerable persons are always the potential beacons of Resurrection Light and so it is that I speak to you on World AIDS Day as to the children of Light who have the task of illuminating the Darkness where Mammon presides and where men and women are so often no more than objects to themselves and to each other.

There are people in this Cathedral today who have come to accept that they may die soon. Would that we had all accepted that we are dying for that is, of course, the truth of the matter. The children of Light live constantly in such certain knowledge and find that it establishes instantly a new order of priorities. Death wonderfully concentrates the mind as Charles I discovered on the eve of his execution; he was then able to write his famous poem that begins with the lines: 'Close thine eyes and sleep secure. Thy soul is safe, thy body sure.' But most of the time we shy away from death because it makes all our strivings for ascendancy over others seem so utterly ridiculous. It expresses the futility of our efforts to create security for ourselves or to amass riches or in some way to become bigshots in the world where Mammon reigns. Robert Maxwell's naked body floating in the water with the eyes open says it all.[1]

Our Lord Jesus is the exemplar of Light in the world. He died at a young age – reviled, tortured, humiliated, blood streaming down a parched and dehydrated body. They had called him all sorts of names – drunkard, sinner, devil-worshipper, blasphemer, womaniser, friend of prostitutes. On him was poured the hatred of the bigots, the condemnation of the self-styled holy men, the fear and contempt of the civic authorities. But this suffering, dying man, nailed to his barbaric cross was and is the Light of the World. He stares death in the face and gives meaning to Life. But he does not die alone for at the foot of the cross are those whose love for him is stronger than their fear of shame or violent arrest. John is there, the beloved apostle who rested on Jesus' breast at supper, Mary his mother with her sister and another Mary and, of course, Mary of Magdala healed of mental illness by Jesus and much beloved by him – the privileged person who was first to encounter the Risen Lord three days later. They are the treasured people with whom Jesus had known the tenderest intimacy and it is this intimacy which sustains him still as death approaches. Seldom was a death more grisly, but never perhaps more intimate.

---

[1] The well-known press magnate had recently died.

I sometimes think of Jesus as the man who died because he was too intimate with others. He even called God, 'Daddy', and he constantly smashed through the interpersonal barriers of the culture of his day. He befriended many women, he mixed with tax collectors, he spoke to Samaritans, he even healed the son of a hated Roman centurion. He dared to be irresistibly attractive as a man and his company was clearly enthralling. He invited intimacy by his very way of being: in him love declared itself constantly and found a ready response. And the world could not bear it. This man, what's more, was no disembodied spirit but vibrant flesh and blood – a man who touched and caressed and took children in his arms. On the night before he went to his death he gave his companions a potent memorial not only of his spiritual teachings but most especially of his incarnate self: he washed their feet, gave them his body and his blood and commanded them to love one another. There could be no clearer proclamation of his incarnate nature and of the fact that divine love is a matter of bodies as well as of souls.

As I call to mind those countless numbers who have died or are now dying of AIDS throughout the world I am drawn inexorably into a Passion story of the twentieth century and see again the excruciating pain of the struggle for intimacy. My fellow human beings, most of them young with their aspirations unfulfilled, are dying because they have contracted a disease that is transmitted through blood and semen. They are dying because they are bodies and in many cases because they yearn for intimacy. They are the representatives of a species that carries still a collective incapacity to relate in ways which bring wholeness and joy and that does not know how to demonstrate with confidence that we are flesh and blood and that we are made for love.

But, dear God, how this excruciating disease is drawing out the poison from the corporate body. The voices of condemnation are shrill in their abuse: sexual and racial prejudice seem ever more rampant: fear and ignorance stalk the land. And then there are those who pass by on the other side – out of fear or contempt or because they believe it has nothing to do with them. But this is the most tragic evasion of all for AIDS is Everyman's and Everywoman's concern and none of us can renounce our membership of the human family by burying our heads in the sand. We are members one of another and it is to those who now struggle with approaching death that we can look for hope. May their love for each other and our love for them strengthen the human race in the quest for true intimacy, which is our destiny. If we are to be the light of the world in an age when tired old Mammon is back on the throne we are called first of all to accept and forgive the depersonalised ones who have fallen into Mammon's maul and to regard with infinite compassion the loss of their humanity. But our forgiveness must be accompanied by a way of being in the world that proclaims that hope lies not in rejection of embodied loving but in its sanctification.

I should like to leave you with the words of Etty Hillesum, a young Dutch Jewish woman who died in Auschwitz and who from 1941 to 1943 kept a diary of her life in Nazi-occupied Amsterdam. For a short while she was in therapy with Julius Spier, the psychochirologist, and then she became his assistant and finally his lover and intellectual partner. Spier died only days before he would have been incarcerated and probably exterminated by the Nazis. Etty's diary entry says all there is to say about being a light in the world and, as she herself was one of the greatest lights to shine in Europe's darkest hour, we do well to listen to her words with our hearts as well as our ears. Of her lover she wrote: 'All the bad and all the good that can be found in a man were in you – all the demons, all the passions, all the goodness, all the love – great discerner, God seeker and God-finder that you were. You sought God in every human heart that opened up before you – and how many there were! – and found a little bit of Him in each one. You never gave up . . .' (Hillesum, 1983, p. 171)

May we likewise never give up so that one day with Our Blessed Lord and Saviour we may be able to cry: 'It is accomplished.'

In the name of the Father, the Son and the Holy Spirit : Amen.

Reference

Hillesum E (1983) Etty: A Diary 1941–43. London: Jonathan Cape Ltd.

Chapter 24
Jesus, the Incarnation of Holiness[1]

Jesus and embodiment (Sunday 10 January 1993)

The Spirit himself joins with our spirit to bear witness that we are children of God. And if we are children, then we are heirs, heirs of God and joint heirs with Christ. (Romans 8: 16–17)

My text is important because it reminds us that any attempt to examine the personality and life of Jesus Christ is by definition to say something about ourselves. Perhaps that is one of the reasons why this last year has seen such a proliferation of books about Jesus – could it be that we are now so preoccupied with trying to understand the mysterious complexity of human nature that theologians and others are inevitably drawn to a re-evaluation of the nature of Jesus himself, the one who has been viewed down the ages as the manifestation of human nature at its most exalted?

Be that as it may, there has certainly been a great deal of media agitation in recent months around a number of books which have appeared about Jesus. Three in particular have hit the headlines: Barbara Thiering's *Jesus the Man – A New Interpretation From the Dead Sea Scrolls,* AN Wilson's *Jesus,* and the latest provocative offering from the Anglican Bishop of Newark, John Spong, entitled *Born of a Woman.* These three books are arguably in a tradition that began in 1906 when Albert Schweitzer wrote his book *The Quest of the Historical Jesus* but what is so fascinating is the way in which such books – often highly eccentric and based on very shaky historical facts let alone theological premises – capture the popular imagination. Jesus, it seems, is still such hot news that AN Wilson's book, for example, can get articles and reviews in every British newspaper while the author himself is invited to appear before millions on TV chat shows and in documentaries. Behind

---

[1]A series of three addresses given in Norwich Cathedral, January 1993.

all this, I believe, is the half-conscious realisation on the part of journalists, readers and viewers alike that Jesus matters because he is the embodiment of hope for humanity. Indeed there are those – A N Wilson, I suspect, among them – who believe that the Church's insistence on making him the Son of God has actually obscured what really matters, namely that Jesus presents us with a human life lived to the full and for that reason offers a continuing and unequalled exemplar.

My three addresses during this Epiphany-tide start from the much more radical, and I would claim, orthodox assumption that we are all sons and daughters of God. That is what defines us; it is the first and last word about our human nature. Jesus exemplifies this truth: he shows us who we are if we can only have the courage to accept the awesome definition of ourselves. Put it another way. Do you remember the words at Jesus' baptism in the River Jordan, 'This is my beloved Son in whom I am well pleased'? Now let those words be whispered in your own ear: 'You are my beloved son (or daughter) in whom I am well pleased.' Can you hear that? Could you ever believe that in the deepest recesses of your own heart? Such is the challenge of our Christian pilgrimage and Jesus goes before us. He accepted his belovedness and because of that he was free to be the person he had it in him to be. What is more, his life, as recorded in the Gospels, gives us an unforgettable picture of what it means to live the life of the beloved. Tonight I want to look briefly with you at his physical embodiment and in the following weeks at his mind and his spirit. And I shall do so with the following questions always in mind: what is it that Jesus, as the beloved of God like me, can show me about myself? And then: can I dare to act on what I am shown?

Bodies are much in the news, too, these days. They are usually abused, tortured, raped or starving bodies. As a therapist for example, I am confronted almost daily with horrific stories, often from the lips of people from so-called respectable middle-class families, of violent physical or sexual abuse, usually perpetrated by close family members, which has left them defenceless victims with a sense of desecration, contamination, of deep impurity. 'I hate my body', they say 'It is dirty, unclean, a source of shame and revulsion.' Others, often women, find themselves caught up in compulsive self-abuse and fall prey to appalling eating disorders, starving themselves and bingeing and purging with obsessive regularity. Truly this seems to be an age where the body is vilified to a degree that is almost beyond belief. At such a time we stand in urgent need of good news about our bodies.

There are those, of course, who cannot bear to think of Jesus' body at all. To do so is somehow for them sacrilegious almost obscene. Certainly for them it is an unholy and unwholesome thing to do. Test yourselves out for a moment by listening to a quotation from Donald Nicholl taken from a book entitled *The Testing of Hearts*. Nicholl, incidentally, is probably best known for his book with the simple title *Holiness*. In this extract he is talking about Jesus in the days after Palm Sunday: 'His feet must have been bruised, for you cannot walk through the Judean Desert barefoot or in sandals without constantly striking your feet against rocks and stones and pebbles. Probably his skin was cracked and likely enough he had fleas on him from riding the donkey. He and his disciples had sweated on the long pull up from Jericho; they must have all smelt of dried sweat since there were no showers in those days and no daily changes of clothes. And we asked ourselves how did they manage to clean themselves after emptying their bowels, since toilet paper and water closets were not yet invented.' But that is all by way of a parenthesis.

What better place to start than Jesus' conception and birth? I wonder if you are asked, as I often am: 'Do you believe in the virgin birth?' For me it feels increasingly to be the wrong question but nonetheless the doctrine points to a deeper truth that gives rise to the right question. 'Do you believe that Jesus was God's son?' To that question I can give a resounding 'yes' and it is a 'yes' that remains quite unaffected by Bishop Spong's theory, for example, that Jesus was, in fact an illegitimate child or even the son of a rapist. Indeed, I can even find some cause for rejoicing in such eccentric ideas for among my clients and acquaintances there are many who are the fruits of such unhappy liaisons and who, as a result, find it impossibly difficult to feel that they are the beloved of God. And yet the conception and birth of Jesus proclaim the essential truth about us all. We are God's children from all eternity and nothing can alter that fact, not even a brutal conception or the experience of an inhospitable womb that never made us welcome. The stories around Jesus' conception and birth proclaim him to be God's love-child – like us and perhaps that does indeed mean he and we are illegitimate – that is beyond the laws of biology. Wordsworth had it right, I believe: 'Trailing clouds of glory do we come from God who is our home.'

A person who is comfortable in his own skin welcomes other bodies and it is precisely this comfortableness that we see in the adult Jesus. Perhaps the most remarkable instance of this occurs at the famous supper in the house of Simon, the pharisee, which we had read to us. You will remember the extraordinary episode when a woman from the town (probably a prostitute) arrives at the supper party and begins kissing and washing his feet with her tears and wiping them with her hair and then anointing them with myrrh. Jesus lets this happen – indeed he commends the woman for honouring his body in a way that Simon his host had neglected to do. Jesus' body is open to the caress of others – remember the moving scene in the garden after the resurrection when he has to curb the instinctive desire of Mary Magdalene to embrace him and cling to him. But, of course, this means that he is also open to wounding. His body is open to love and to treachery – to the embrace of Mary and the kiss of Judas, to the glory of the Transfiguration and to the desolation of the cross.

Jesus, it seems, permitted his body to be cherished and to be abused but it would be utterly wrong to see him always in the passive role. It is clear that he in turn stretched out to others and in doing so often brought healing and life. In brief, we see in Jesus what it means to be truly at home in the body; there is no inhibition and no defensiveness but rather a preparedness to receive and to bestow tenderness and benediction. There is no sign of that misuse of the body that seeks to assert power and domination. There is, rather, a total absence of the characteristic male aggressiveness that in our culture is often associated with sexual prowess and the act of penetration. It is only a fundamental contempt for the body that leads a person to use his body to subjugate and humiliate another. Jesus shows us that our embodiment, far from being the channel for violence and aggression, can be the means of communion and the source of community, a community, incidentally, which includes not only all those other human beings in the world but all the physical organisms of the universe. I do not believe it is fanciful to suggest that there is a deep connection between the cherishing of our bodies and our care of planet Earth.

What, then, do we learn from Jesus, the incarnation of holiness whose body, like ours, was divinely wrought? We learn to celebrate our embodiment and to know our bodies as channels for the expression of love and blessing. We learn not to be afraid of being openly acceptant and responsive despite the wounds that will inevitably come. Above all we learn that our bodies yearn to participate in the reciprocal exchange of tenderness and that it is through such activity that the body of Christ, that is the Church, can find holiness and wholeness. It is not by chance that the night before he died Jesus took bread and wine and said: 'This is my body, this is my blood.' Could ever a message be clearer?

References

Nicholl D (1981) Holiness. London: Darton, Longman & Todd.
Nicholl D (1989) The Testing of Hearts. London: Lamp Press.
Schweitzer A (1906, 1954) The Quest of the Historical Jesus. London: A & C Black.
Spong JS (1992) Born of a Woman. San Francisco, CA: Harper Collins.
Thiering B (1992) Jesus the Man: A New Interpretation from the Dead Sea Scrolls. London: Doubleday.
Wilson AN (1992) Jesus. London: Sinclair-Stevenson.

The mind of Jesus (Sunday 17 January 1993)

After three days they found him sitting in the temple surrounded by the teachers, listening to them and putting questions; and all who heard him were amazed at his intelligence and the answers he gave. (Luke 2: 46–48)

On these three Sunday evenings, fired by the recent flood of books on the personality of Jesus, I am offering some reflections on the nature of the man whom Christians believe to be the incarnate Son of God and on the implications for us who are his brothers and sisters. Last week we thought about Jesus as a physical being. Tonight I want to reflect for a while on the mind of Jesus.

Let me be clear at the outset that what I mean by mind in this context is the capacity to think and to feel, to deploy reason, imagination and intuition and to communicate through the use of language. Interestingly enough we probably have more detailed information about this aspect of Jesus' personality than any other. Modern biblical scholarship has been divided about how we should view the Gospels – are they to be treated as biographies or are they actually theological faith documents written to instruct first century Christians? The consensus now seems to be that they are, in fact, both; that is to say, they are theologically reflective biographies. But however we view them it is clear that they depend for their content to a very large extent on the reported or interpreted or explicated sayings and conversations of Jesus. We may not know what Jesus looked like, whether he was handsome or ugly, short or tall, but we do know how he thought and felt and how his words and discourses reverberated in the consciousness of his followers.

The episode in the Temple, which was read to us tonight, is only recorded by Luke and it is so striking that is seems unlikely to be narrator's licence on the evangelist's part simply to make a theological point. Jesus, it is clear was an exceptionally bright 12-year-old. Not only did he have a firm sense of his own identity (and I will return to this next week) but he had a mind of his own and was utterly fearless in debate. Such fearlessness was not the outcome of precocious arrogance; we are told that Jesus listened as well as posed questions. Indeed, it is fair to assume that he did much listening during his boyhood and adolescence for it is clear during his later adult ministry that he is steeped in the scriptures and in the law. When he went to the Temple at the age of 12 he was already deeply knowledgeable and such knowledge could only have resulted from dedicated study and deep attentiveness to the precious inheritance of his culture and tradition. It is not fanciful, I believe, to see in the 12-year-old Jesus a boy whose self-confidence was the result of his disciplined willingness to listen to the teachers of his day and to treasure the accumulated wealth of his culture. These, then, are not the signs of arrogance but rather of the hunger and thirst for the knowledge that leads to wisdom.

Throughout the Gospel accounts the evidence abounds that Jesus is continually drawing from a well-stocked mind. But he is no arid scholar. On the contrary he is a consummate storyteller and he shows himself to have great imaginative gifts that are nourished by his acute observation of the world about him. The parables of Jesus are, in fact, exquisite works of art. Their material is drawn from everyday life – often the worlds of agriculture and commerce – but Jesus fashions the material so that it takes on great symbolic power, which has the effect of startling his listeners and often disturbing them by touching on deep feelings and prejudices. This capacity to communicate in profound and unexpected ways reveals another central facet of Jesus' mind. He has an extraordinary ability to empathise with others – to enter into their perception of reality and, as a result, to offer them comfort or, when he so chooses, to shake them ruthlessly out of their complacency. Contrast, for example, the effect on different listeners of the story of the Pharisee and the Publican going up to the Temple to pray. If you were a much-maligned tax-gatherer you could gain deep comfort from the story but if you were a Pharisee you would be shaken, even enraged, by what you heard. In brief, Jesus uses his intellectual acuity, his imagination and his empathy to enter into relationships fearlessly; he is afraid neither of intimacy nor of conflict and his mind, trained and disciplined as it is, is freely exercised in the service of both.

Imagine if you will, then, the impact of this man on those who came into close contact with him. He is knowledgeable, imaginative, a great storyteller, deeply empathic and, above all, he is wonderfully articulate: he uses language at its most richly expressive – similes and images come tumbling from his lips but he can also tease and mystify. What is more he has a wry sense of humour and can talk of rich men struggling like camels to get through the eyes of needles and of people walking around with planks of wood in their eyes. So great, indeed, is his capacity to use language that he seems by turn to be storyteller, poet, philosopher, theologian, lawyer, preacher, educator, healer and intimate friend. He seems equally at home with large crowds, small groups, and in close encounters with individuals. He is able to hold an assembly of thousands spellbound and draw individuals to him by the mere utterance of their name. However we view the historic and factual accuracy of the Gospels, there can be no doubt that the Jesus they present is a man of formidable mind who uses language with effortless artistry. Like all great minds, he knew, too, the compelling power of silence. If we were to use modern terminology, we might describe him as nourished by the left and right hemispheres of his brain and open equally to the masculine and the feminine sides of his personality.

It is not often, I believe, that we are encouraged to focus on the mind of Jesus in this way. On the contrary it is not uncommon for him to be presented as a straightforward, uncomplicated person whose holiness is characterised by a child-like simplicity and innocence. Nothing could be further from the truth. It is, of course, the case that Jesus commends a childlike attitude of receptive trust and challenges those who deploy their cleverness in order to trip others up or to humiliate them. But his own way of being in the world demonstrates repeatedly that his was a rich and agile mind dedicated to his Father's business every moment of the day. For Jesus language is holy; words are sacraments of love and healing and they can also be destroyers of pretence, hypocrisy and self-deception. But they matter inordinately.

For us, his brothers and sisters, the mind of Jesus confronts us with the challenge of our own expressive potential. Of course, we cannot all be great thinkers nor do we all possess the ability to be orators or story-tellers. But how seriously do we take the gifts of language and of under-standing which most of us possess abundantly? How often do we visit the treasure-house of our own cultural and religious heritage and seek to appropriate its riches? How assiduously do we seek to be replenished by the great teachers and writers of our own and past generations? How concerned are we to be fully attentive to and observant to others' real-ities so that we can enter into their inner worlds? How concerned are we to develop those imaginative faculties that our technological age threatens to extinguish and without which the world of symbols loses its power to nourish and awaken us? And, finally, do we dare to believe that our words can be sacraments of healing and that our words can draw evil into the open and destroy it?

The answer to all these questions must ultimately depend on whether or not we share in the 'Father's business' that determined both the development and the activity of the mind of Jesus. Are we, like him, committed to Kingdom values and to the extension of the Kingdom and not to the outward form of things?

For me, one of the most glorious examples of the mind of Jesus in action is provided by the story of his meeting with the Samaritan woman at the well.[1] To start with, for him to talk with a Samaritan woman at all was an unheard of breach of convention. (The disciples, we are told, were 'greatly surprised'). After asking her for a drink, Jesus plunges into a theological conversation which is a delicate and profound verbal dance. Both of them, it seems, revel in the quality of cut and thrust which characterises their dialogue. And then, as the woman takes a step forward in her understanding of the engaging stranger, Jesus suddenly tells her to go and call her husband and then come back.

There is something mischievously teasing about this because Jesus, so great is his empathy and insight, has already intuited the woman's life history. 'I haven't got a husband', she says. She doesn't appear defensive and she clearly wants to go on with the conversation. But she must have wondered what was coming next. When Jesus speaks again, there is not condemnation – rather a kind of humorous, almost approving comment. 'You're telling the truth there', Jesus says. 'You've had five husbands and the man you're living with is not really your husband.' Now, of course, there's no way we shall ever know what happened to her five husbands

---

[1] John 4: 7–30.

but it's a fair guess that for all five marriages to have ended in death is beyond all reasonable odds, even given the poor standard of health and hygiene in first century Palestine! But Jesus makes no comment on the fact that she is currently cohabiting with a man and seems distinctly uninterested in the form of her personal relationships in the past or in the present. As far as we know she is not subsequently asked to repent or change her living arrangements. Indeed, she is wildly excited and tells her neighbours. 'He told me everything I have ever done.' The mind of Jesus has seen her as she is, has accepted her as she is and, as a result, she is enabled to believe in the Kingdom and to tell others about it. What really mattered to Jesus was that she could receive the Water of Life. A mind about the 'Father's business' is uncluttered by inessentials and loves the intimacy of transparent truthfulness. That is the mind of Jesus and we are challenged to become like him. 'In the beginning was the Word and the Word was with God and the Word was God.'

The spirit of Jesus (Sunday 24 January 1993)

Anyone who has seen me has seen the Father. (John 14: 9)

Tonight, in the last of these three addresses on the personality of Jesus, I want to get to the heart of this extraordinary man, the core of him, the essence of this being whom the Church calls God. This is what I mean by 'spirit'. My spirit and your spirit is what ultimately defines us: it is our spirit that gives meaning and direction to our existence, it is our spirit that determines our identity and it is our spirit which bears the mark of immortality. We are body, mind and spirit but it is the spirit that breathes life and gives light – or colludes with death and darkness. The existentialist's question: 'Who am I?' can only be satisfactorily answered in terms of spirit.

Last week we saw Jesus at the age of 12 debating in the Temple. You will remember his astonishing self-assurance and the utter confidence in his own identity. This was a boy who knew what he had to do and was apparently surprised that his parents did not possess similar insight. He gently chides them for being anxious on his account and for not realising that he had to be in his Father's house. The significance of this psychological landscape cannot be exaggerated. Jesus lived, as it were, in communion with his heavenly Father and his whole mode of being in the world was the outcome of this relationship. So complete was this relationship that he was able to say later to his disciples: 'He who has seen me has seen the Father.' In other words he claimed that the relationship with his Father determined the nature of his own being and was, indeed, the essence of his identity.

How, we might legitimately ask, was this relationship conducted? I believe the Gospels give us plenty of clues. Clearly Jesus prayed. We are told that he withdrew from the crowds to pray; we hear of his sojourn in the wilderness; we read of the agonising conversation with his Father in the Garden. Jesus related to his Father in the depths of his own being: at the centre of his own inner self he found his Father. 'The Father and I are one.' One, yes, but at the same time two – a duality that is transcended by the love between them – and there, I suggest, we have the doctrine of the Holy Trinity. But it was not only in prayer that Jesus entered into communion with his Father. It would seem that he found this Father, too, in the created world around him – in other people and in the natural order. For Jesus, his Father was to be met both within his own being and outside of himself but – and this is the fundamental issue – it was this meeting, this continuing communion which permeated his whole life. And it was because of this that he becomes our salvation for he shows us the way to enter into the hidden mystery of the Godhead. To enter into the spirit of Jesus is to share his knowledge and his passionate love of the Father. Jesus, fully human and whole and holy, enables us, his brothers and sisters, to be drawn into the mystery that is the Father. The summit of the Christian religion is contained in those remarkable words that come later in John's Gospel: 'As you, Father, are in me and I in you, may they also be in us . . . I in them and you in me, that they may be completely one.'

Who was this Father with whom Jesus was in deep communion at the centre of his own being? If we wish to penetrate the spirit of Jesus then we are challenged to draw near to this Father. I am intrigued that in the whole of the Gospels there are only seven words preserved for us from the language that Jesus actually spoke – Aramaic. And significantly one of those words is the name by which Jesus addressed his Father – Abba. This is the language of intimacy, of the child talking to daddy. This is a very different God from the Yahweh of the Old Testament who was so much to be revered that it was not even safe to name him. With the God of the Old Testament there was always the fear of judgement and consequently the need for the Law to be kept at all costs. Jesus shows us a very different Father with whom he is intimately at home and with whom he feels totally at one.

Perhaps you are wondering what the other six Aramaic words are from the recorded sayings of Jesus. In fact, they tell us much more about the Father. Do you remember 'Talitha cumi', 'Little girl, I say to you arise'? For me there is something overpoweringly beautiful about the story of Jairus' daughter.[2] Jairus, you will recall, was the president of one of the synagogues - an important man - but what we know about him is that he loved his daughter profoundly. He could not bear that she should die. And he throws himself at Jesus' feet and pleads with him to

[2]Matthew 9: 18–27.

heal his sick little girl. Jesus goes with Jairus and, as he goes, the hem of his garment is touched by a woman in the crowd who has suffered from haemorrhages for twelve years. Jesus is immediately aware that power has gone out of him and turns to discover the woman whose faith is so great. 'Daughter', he says, 'your faith has cured you.' Is it not strange that Jesus should call her daughter for in all probability she was older than he was? I would suggest that Jesus, moved profoundly by the passionate love of Jairus for his daugher, is on fire with the power of his Father's healing love. The woman with the haemorrhage has only to touch his clothes for that love to be immediately effective. A little while later Jesus arrives at Jairus' house and, with Jairus at his side, he takes hold of the hand of the little girl who is now dead: 'Talitha cumi.' The love and power of the Father pours out of him – and we can imagine that Jairus, too, adds his own passionate love – and the little girl immediately gets up and, delightfully, she walks about. Mark adds, seemingly as an after-thought, 'She was twelve years old' – the age when Jesus was about his Father's business in the Temple and the same number of years that the woman with the haemorrhage had suffered.

This, then, is the Father with whom Jesus is in constant communion: he is a Father of indescribable love and power who cares passionately for his children. It is as if Jairus, the human father, so intuits the power of the heavenly Father residing in Jesus that he knows that simply Jesus' presence will radiate healing and life. It is as if Jesus is proclaiming to the whole world: 'Talitha cumi'

The other four Aramaic words are very different: 'Eloi, eloi, lama sabachthani?' 'My God, my God, why have you forsaken me?' On the cross Jesus, it seems, loses touch with his beloved Father. No longer does he call him 'Abba' but he reverts to the Hebrew form 'Eloi' or 'Elohim', the Old Testament God of judgement. For one terrible moment, it seems, Jesus despairs; he is no longer in contact with the depths of his own being, his whole identity trembles – the beloved Father has abandoned him. I have come to believe that in this moment of terrible agony Jesus is restored to his Father's arms by the love of his mother and his friends. Mary, Mary Magdalene and John were there, and resting in their gaze and bathed in their love Jesus rediscovers the core of his own being and is united once more to his Father. 'It is finished! Father into your hands I commend my spirit.'

I want to leave you with the most wonderful picture of God the Father that the world has ever been given – the father in the story of the Prodigal Son, which we heard this evening.[3]

It is so easy to become caught up in the personalities of the sons in this extraordinary story that we fail to make the father the centre of our attention. It is perhaps easier to see the prodigal in ourselves or perhaps,

[3] Luke 15: 11–32.

more likely, if we are faithful churchgoers, the elder son. But Jesus tells us that, because we are like him, it is really the Father whom we have dwelling in our own hearts. Is that remotely credible? Could it be that we are not only the beloved sons and daughters with whom the Father is well pleased but that we also have it within us to become like the Father himself? Perhaps the most incredible statement Jesus ever made is: 'Be compassionate as your Father is compassionate.' Can we really become like that? It means that we are called to accept others unconditionally, to have nothing to do with the exercise of power, to welcome sinners home, to renounce a competitive lifestyle, to commit ourselves to an absolute compassion in which no trace of condemnation can be found. The spirit of Jesus invites us to become like the heavenly Father and to see the world through his grief-stricken, forgiving, generous eyes. In brief, we are challenged to give up our dependency and our childish self-gratification and to carry the responsibility of being adult spiritual persons who welcome home life's wounded pilgrims and love them with a passionate intensity. 'Father', said Jesus, 'they do not belong to the world any more than I belong to the world . . . may they all be one . . . just as, Father, you are in me and I am in you, so that they also may be in us, so that the world may believe it was you who sent me.'

Chapter 25
A Sermon Preached in King's College Chapel Cambridge[1]

Every man heard them speak in his own language. (Acts 2: 6)

The verses from Acts[2] that were read a few minutes ago are indelibly printed upon my memory because they were the first Bible passage I had to read aloud as a child in church. What is more the reading was landed on me at two minutes' notice because of another child's illness. I was only 10 at the time and I can still remember my horror at being confronted by the seemingly endless list of strange names and countries, none of which I really knew how to pronounce. Phrygia and Pamphilia nearly saw my come-uppance and what a relief it was to arrive at 'the wonderful works of God' with all those strange names now blessedly behind me for better or for worse.

Today the passage fills me with overwhelming excitement. It's a good job I am here in King's Chapel where the superb architecture, liturgy and music will ensure that I do not break into glossolalia or throw myself ecstatically on the floor. Indeed if I were to do so I would be behaving like a barbarian in the royal court and would in any case be offending against my own nature and against the Law of Hospitality. I shall not, I assure you, speak in tongues, nor shall I roll on the carpet but I want passionately, if I can, to speak in your language and in mine and to discover that they might just possibly be the same.

Is it not an amazing experience to hear someone speak in one's own language? I don't mean the often distressing experience of hearing the complaining tones of a sophisticated Oxbridge person in the middle of a vegetable market in Tamilnadu. I am thinking of the magical moment of hearing the words of a person who through his or her communication tells me that I am known and understood and that because of this we can enter a conversation of intimacy. The amazement of the Phrygians, the

---

[1] This sermon was given at the 10.30 a.m. Eucharist on 18 May 1997, the Feast of Pentecost.
[2] Acts 2: 1–11

Pamphilians and all the rest of them was that they felt instantly recognised, related to and communicated with in a way that electrified their minds and hearts. This language that they heard went to the very core of their being and they knew that it was transforming. Not all of them you may remember – there were those who cynically observed that the apostles were drunk but we are told that they were mockers, that is to say denigrators of their fellow human-beings, holding them in contempt, and presumably therefore, as modern psychology would tell us, caught up in self-contempt.

It seems that on this long-ago day of Pentecost, which heralded the new era in the history of the world, language was not a problem. Communication was immediate and profound, there was no impediment to relationship and in this astounding openness of mind-to-mind and heart-to-heart the wonderful works of God were manifest.

And yet, and yet – despite their amazement, the extraordinarily heterogeneous crowd in Jerusalem on that momentous day were in doubt. In bewilderment they asked themselves and each other 'What does this mean?' The mockers were openly cynical but the others, despite being caught up as they were in an extraordinary experience of being communicated to in their personal language, were at first also troubled. It was all too good to be true: they doubted even though they were 'devout men'.

Can we do any better? That depends, I suppose, whether we believe that this self-same Spirit that descended with such startling power on the day which has come to be known as the Church's birthday is still operative and will lead us into all truth. I cannot hope to be a Peter who stood up and spoke with such clarity and conviction to the crowd in Jerusalem that day. What I can do, though, is to tell you why I am excited and what I have glimpsed of that truth that may yet save us from ourselves and from destruction.

First, the Spirit tells me that the other need not be alien to me, he or she need not be an inscrutable mystery, a dark unknown. On the contrary, if I did but know it we speak the same language at the core of our beings. He or she may be of different gender, of different race, of different colour, of different religion. But we are both wondrously made and our needs and desires are the same. If we lose our fear of each other, listen attentively to each other, little by little we shall hear each other's words and know that we speak a common language. Not easy in our risk-phobic culture where we spend so much time worrying about insurance and litigation. It becomes increasingly difficult even to approach another person without being perceived as a potential seducer or abuser. Second, the Spirit tells me that I must let go of mockery and contempt – both of others and myself. And I must do so because not to do so is to commit blasphemy. If God pours out His Spirit on all humankind, who am I to throw back this generous and infinite love in His face? Persistent self-blame and self recrimination are not the marks of humility: they are the hallmark of a stubborn resistance to Infinite Love and as such they keep me from myself, from my brothers and sisters and from the God who loves me.

Third, the Spirit tells me that the essential truth about humankind is that we are all members one of another. We belong to the same family that stretches through time and space and eternity. The message of Pentecost is that we are all united in one bond and fellowship and there is nothing we can do to change that truth, however much we twist and turn and however vilely we treat each other.

We are born so that we may claim our intimacy with each other and know that we are infinitely beloved. Then we can take our place in the human family knowing that to be fully ourselves is to claim our birthright. Is this the language that, if we can but hear it, may yet save us? I believe it is, and what is more I begin to hear it faintly beneath the turbulence of our national life in the last three weeks. Two days after the General Election, Donald Nicholl, the outstanding Catholic layman, historian and spiritual writer died. He it was who in 1993 wrote of a conversation he had recently had with a Palestinian liberation theologian. 'Do you in Britain', asked the theologian, 'need a theology of liberation?' 'Yes', Donald answered. 'Then what do you need to be liberated from?' he continued. 'The answer I gave to my friend', said Donald, 'came to me spontaneously, without conscious premeditation, in one word. Even to myself it was a surprise. I said: "Contempt".'[3] Contempt which Donald saw all around him in the Britain of 1993 remains the implacable enemy of the Spirit that it always was. It threatens to stifle the Holy Spirit of God which uncovers our common language, reveals the tenderness of intimacy and restores us to our uniqueness and to our profound interconnectedness. Donald, it seems, was ready to move on to the next stage of his pilgrimage for in his diary entry for 30 January of this year he wrote: 'I have received intimations of what this "new creation" might be, and what it might be to love unconditionally – I need to be bathed in the unconditional love of God which is heaven, plunged in the ocean of pure love. I have a longing for that boundless love, which would prove to be a constant ache if I were restored now to bodily health'.[4] My prayer for us all this Pentecost is that we may find the common language which is ours by right as children of the same family and that the discovery will create in us so constant an ache that we shall be forced to pray with passionate intensity: 'Thy kingdom come on earth, as it is in heaven.' And, as we pray, we shall know with assurance that we speak the language of Jesus – Christ, Our Lord, our friend, our passionate redeemer who longs for us to acknowledge who we truly are.

---

[3] Quoted in *The Tablet*, 9 May 1997.
[4] Quoted in *The Tablet*, 9 May 1997.

Postscript

The publication of this book marks a transition in my own life. On 31 December 1997, after 30 years as a person-centred counsellor in higher education, I stepped down from my post as Director of Counselling in the University of East Anglia. Although I continue to work as a therapist in an industrial setting and remain heavily involved in the training of counsellors, there is undoubtedly a new sense of space, even of liberation, in my life. Such freedom, however, brings with it new decisions to face and new commitments to undertake. I am currently in good health and can reasonably look forward to another decade of productive living.

Bringing together earlier work for inclusion in this volume has revealed to me the emerging pattern of my own professional and spiritual development. It seems that in a way that is sometimes surprising I am 'coming home'. For me, as I see it, my work as a person-centred therapist has been a passionate and wholly appropriate part of a pilgrimage that has as its goal the claiming of my birthright as both the lover and the beloved of God. I suppose, if I am honest, person-centred therapy has afforded me the most remarkable opportunity to pursue this path in a world that is often deaf to the claims of the spiritual traditions of our ancestors and apparently cut off from the life-giving and healing power of the language, symbols and ritual of those traditions. I am not convinced, however, that such alienation is permanent. What is more, I fear that unless, as a culture, we can rediscover the well-springs and the spiritual nourishment of which we stand in need we may well perish for lack of them. I know that I am coming home to the place where I first started and I await expectantly the outcome of recognising that place afresh or perhaps for the first time. True to my person-centred discipline that, for me, is as sacred as any religious rule of life, I shall attempt to trust the mysterious process and not to be afraid.

Name index

Subject index